JANICE T. CONNELL

◼

MARY, QUEEN of ANGELS

◼

Answers to
Universal
Questions

MJF BOOKS
NEW YORK

Published by MJF Books
Fine Communications
322 Eighth Avenue
New York, NY 10001

Mary, Queen of Angels
LC Control Number: 2003107635
ISBN-13: 978-1-56731-595-0
ISBN-10: 1-56731-595-X

QM   10   9   8   7   6

Hear and let it penetrate into your heart, my dear little son: let nothing discourage you, nothing depress you. Let nothing alter your heart or your countenance. Also do not fear any illness and vexation, anxiety or pain. Am I not here who am your mother? Are you not under my shadow and protection? Am I not your fountain of life? Are you not in the folds of my mantle, in the crossing of my arms? Is there anything else that you need?

—*Words of Our Lady of Guadalupe,*
to Juan Diego, Dec. 12, 1531

Acknowledgments

To all of the following who brought this book to life, I remain eternally grateful.

The Lord, who allowed me the privilege of authoring this book. The Mother of Jesus, whose love has inspired me throughout my life.

My family, living and deceased, whose kindness touches every page. *Mary, Queen of Angels* reflects insights, sacrifices, and loving contributions of my husband, Edward, and children and grandchildren.

The inspiration for this book belongs to Robert Faricy, S.J., S.T.D. His leadership, scholarship, and discernment are reflected throughout the book. Roman Danylak, D.D., Thomas Forrest, C.S.S.R., S.T.D., Leo O'Donovan, S.J., S.T.D., Thomas King, S.J. Ph.D., Adrien Van Kaam, C.S.Sp., Ph.D., Michael Scanlan, T.O.R., J.D., Thomas Thompson, S.M., Ph.D., Msgr. Thomas Duffy, Alexander de Costa Fernandes, OSB, Roderick Jones, OSB, Lucy Rooney, S.N.D. de N., S.T.L., Sisters of Our Lady of Grace and Compassion, OSB, especially Sister Superior Virginia Sebastion, the Sisters of Our Lady of Mount Carmel, especially Mother Theresa Margaret of Lafayette, LA. The Hon. Margaret M. Heckler J.D., M. Jenkins Cromwell, Jr. J.D., Dennis Owen, Susan Muto, Ph.D., W. Shepherdson Abell, J.D. and Kathryn Abell, and John and Ishbel McGregor for their inspiring dedication to the Mother of God, and for their expertise, discernment and encouragement, all of which find expression in this book.

G. Joel Fotinos was highly chosen by name to guide and edit *Mary, Queen of Angels*. May his wisdom bring blessings of peace and light. Denise Silvestro served as a true daughter of the Queen of Angels. May her generosity be a sign for these times and all times. The staff at Penguin Putnam responded with heroic dedication to *Mary, Queen of Angels*.

Bob Angelotti, Faithful Knight of the Queen of Angels, brings this book to the world. May his path be clear and his friends be faithful.

Loving friends and confidantes of the Queen of Angels have helped me to prepare this book. They deserve our deepest gratitude.

Any mistakes or errors are totally due to my inadequacies.

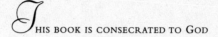

THIS BOOK IS CONSECRATED TO GOD

IN CHRIST'S NAME

WITH DEEP LOVE AND GRATITUDE

FOR THE GIFT OF THE QUEEN OF ANGELS

AND HER CELESTIAL COURT.

IT IS DEDICATED TO THE FULFILLMENT

OF GOD'S WILL

FOR THE HUMAN RACE.

Contents

CHAPTER THREE: KEYS TO CURES

CHAPTER FOUR: KEYS TO HEALING

Part Two: Finding Paradise

MARY,
QUEEN *of*
ANGELS

Author's Note

Mary shows us God. To find peace and purpose in these times, we need to be able to see God, to know God, to be one with God. Prior to the Second Coming of Christ, as He did in the early Church, Jesus sends Mary to open our eyes, our ears, and our hearts. Jesus proclaimed in His Sermon on the Mount: Blessed are the pure of heart for they shall see God. Mary's sole mission is to bring us into the presence of God.

The cultural, social, political, economic, and spiritual changes of the last one hundred fifty years mandate feminine illumination for the third millennium. Mary has answers we all need now to universal questions that impact each of us. Mary, our priceless feminine spiritual legacy, is a worldwide cultural icon of holiness and wholeness. She is a living sign of God's presence among us. Mary shows us how to be happy, how to discover what God wants us to do with our lives.

Technology is the language of life now. We are all more than the eye sees. So also the planet we inhabit and the cosmos around us. Although change is never easy for anyone, the rapid growth of the information super hi-way shows us that we are all interconnected not only technologically but also emotionally, psychologically, materially, and spiritually.

This is my seventh book about Mary. During extensive research, I have discovered amazing facts and events from people of all walks of life, with different political, social, economic, national backgrounds and religious affiliations. The investigation is a process that is ongoing and growing. My work continues to uncover new dimensions of Mary's role in history and in our modern world.

Mary is a celebration of all human cultures steeped in faith. Mary reveals spiritual values that sustain us and give us hope. Men and women throughout the world find in Mary the highest elements within us that motivate us to embrace the whole human race as born of the one true God.

We are each challenged to know and appropriate the mysteries and ways of Almighty God, who created the universe and later sent His Son, Jesus Christ, to earth to redeem humankind by becoming man, being born of a woman, Mary, His Mother. The special role that Mary occupies in the life and mission of Jesus is the subject of much of my life's work. In previous books, I have chronicled historical events involving Mary. It may be helpful to relate some of these events here as a backdrop and foundation to this book about Mary as Queen of Angels.

The Queen of Angels belongs not only to certain Judeo-Christians, but to all God's people. This fact was manifested several years ago in a most dramatic way during the tour for my book *Meetings With Mary*. Arriving at a large bookstore in a shopping mall in Texas, I noticed an inordinate number of pick-up trucks with attached gun racks in the parking lot. Inside, waiting for my lecture that evening, were upwards of fifty men, dressed in jeans, plaid shirts, and boots, swarthy, and in their mid-thirties to mid-forties. I was astounded at the sheer number of robust men (without wives or children) in attendance.

Someone volunteered that none of the men or others present was Catholic. No one had ever heard of the apparitions of Mary during the last fifteen years in Akita or Venezuela or Rwanda or Argentina. I thought I had come to the wrong place.

One of the men stood up and told an extraordinary story. He explained to the entire group that he was a Protestant, and during the afternoon, as he worked in a local sawmill, Mary, the Mother of Jesus Christ, appeared to him. He was quite forthright as he said: "I told the vision to go away, in the name of Jesus Christ, my Lord and Savior. She smiled saying, 'My Son, who is God, has sent me, His Mother, to you so that you may truly know Him. I am Queen of Angels, and I am gathering the flock of my Son.'

"I got afraid and told her again to leave, saying, 'I can never call you Mother of God.'"

"Did she go away?" I asked the man. His eyes suddenly filled with tears, his rough hands unconsciously folded in prayer as he bowed his head. "The Beautiful Lady from Heaven said to me, 'It matters not what you call me. Love my Son, serve my Son, be like my Son.'"

"Why did you come here tonight?" I asked. He responded, "The Beautiful Lady from Heaven told me to come here, and to bring these other men . . ."

Many wonderful gifts from the Heart of God's Love flowed to all of us that evening. As I mentioned the story of Mary's apparition to St. Bernadette Soubirous at Lourdes, someone jumped from his chair and strenuously challenged me: "M'am, where *exactly* does the Bible refer to Mary as the 'Immaculate Conception'?" Praying immediately for the help of the Holy Spirit, I heard myself say: "Sir, do turn to Luke 1:28 through 29."

The hearty man whipped his New Testament from his hip pocket and read aloud the words of the Archangel Gabriel to Mary: "Hail, full of grace . . ." Something happened to him and to all of us as he said those words.

"Full of grace. . . ." he slowly repeated. "*Gratia plena.* Not just a little grace, like us—she was full of grace!" he said, almost in a whisper. Time froze and we were caught up into the presence of the Lord among us. When the manager informed us that he was locking the doors for the night, we realized that the evening at the bookstore had passed in the blink of an eye.

Mary's universal significance was demonstrated to me at another bookstore event. Mother Teresa of Calcutta touched my life in a most dramatic way. I wrote about that encounter in the book *Praying with Mary.* During a lecture about the book at a bookstore in an affluent suburb of Washington, D.C., I noticed in the audience a large group of men and women attired in the traditional garb of their native India. They were listening intently. Some were openly weeping as I told them story after story of Mary's intercessory power on our behalf in the Kingdom of God.

After the lecture, one of the women quietly asked me, "Did Mary, the Mother of God, reincarnate among our people in India?" Her question led me to explain that Christians do not believe in reincarnation. She continued: "Could Mother

Teresa of Calcutta be the reincarnation of Mary? Look what she has done for our people! She truly is the Queen of Angels." Her search for truth about the Queen of Angels mirrors the quest in every human heart.

Many Americans are keenly aware of at least the cultural role of Mary Queen of Angels. The first archbishop of the American colonies, John Carroll, consecrated the nation to her before the Declaration of Independence and the Constitution were signed.

Earlier, on November 23, 1753, young Major George Washington, who is believed to be among the first white men to set foot in the forest now known as Pittsburgh, Pennsylvania, arrived with dispatches to the commander of French troops stationed at a fort in the vicinity. He discovered a chapel erected at Fort Duquesne, located at the confluence of the Allegheny and Monongahela Rivers, which merge to form the Ohio River at that point. It was dedicated to the Mother of God under the title "The Assumption of the Blessed Virgin Mary of the Beautiful River." Today, near this site, stands an ancient and much-beloved church frequented by people from all over the world, which is familiarly known as "Old Saint Mary's of the Point."

Even earlier, in 1531, at Mexico City, at daybreak on a cold, dreary hilltop that once housed a temple to the mother-goddess of the Aztecs,

Mary's presence was witnessed. Poverty-stricken widower Juan Diego, whose name in the Aztec tribe was Nahuatl (Singing Eagle), encountered the Queen of Angels standing before him on Tepeyac Hill. She was encased in the dazzling beauty of Heaven and surrounded by rays of light as bright as the noonday sun, with the moon beneath her feet. She wore a gown of crimson and gold, and a blue mantle bespangled with stars covered her head, cascading down over her dress in graceful folds. Juan Diego knew the Queen of Angels was the Mother of God and Spiritual Mother of the human race when she said to him:

My dear little son, I love you. I desire you to know who I am. I am the ever-virgin Mary, Mother of the True God, who gives life and maintains it in existence. I desire all people to experience my compassion. All those who sincerely ask my help in their work and in their sorrows will know my Mother's Heart. . . . I will see their tears; I will console them and they will experience peace. . . . Do not be distressed and afraid. Am I not here with you who am your Mother? Are you not under my shadow and protection? . . . One day all God's people will know my love for you and all my little children. My little son, I am your Mother. Do not fear.

Much earlier, during the lives of the apostles of Jesus Christ, a most amazing and foundational event occurred that gives us some understanding of Mary's title, Queen of Angels. Every subsequent generation has truly been inspired by the following event.

Saint James the apostle was unsuccessfully preaching the Gospel to unbelieving natives of Caesar Augusta, now known as Saragossa, or Santiago de Compostela. Today, this area, located in the northwestern corner of Spain, is one of the most sacred destinations in the world. Little wonder, for James the apostle discovered no one there was then interested in Jesus Christ. No one listened to him. In desperation, the rejected apostle knelt on the bank of the River Ebro in deep prayer. Surrounded by hard-hearted pagans who laughed at his fervor, mocked his faith, and threatened to kill him, James prayed mightily for divine guidance.

A deep loneliness for the Lord Jesus overtook the apostle. He well knew that the Blessed Mother and the other apostles were in Jerusalem at the time. Would he be able to escape this dangerous place and return there? Would he ever see the people he loved again?

James had been with Jesus on the Mount of Transfiguration where he saw Jesus, surrounded with the glories of Heaven, speaking to Moses and Elijah. James was also present when Jesus suffered His agony in the garden. He saw Jesus sweat blood, betrayed by one of His own, arrested, tortured, and crucified. James, fearing for his own safety now, was uncertain what his next step should be.

Quite suddenly, James saw the Mother of Jesus Christ in the sky. She was seated on a jasper pillar and surrounded by a multitude of angels who were silently transporting her toward him.* Amazed and overjoyed, but still heartbroken, James fell to the ground. Dazzling in the Light of the Resurrected Christ, Mary was attired in resplendent garments, and her crown, studded with sparkling gems, sent glistening rays in every color of the rainbow over the ripples of the dark river. The angels modestly withdrew as their Queen spoke quietly to her Son's apostle.

History tells us that Mary, as Queen of Angels, brought powerful graces that day to James for the people of Spain. Mary reminded the apostle that he was, in fact, a pillar of the church of Jesus Christ. The Queen of Angels identified Spain as a place where the faith would permanently rest. She imparted special blessings to her Spanish children of all generations. The Queen of Angels profoundly inspired James the apostle to carry out her Son's command to make disciples of the people of all nations.

James, by now on fire with renewed faith, trust, and love, was thereafter able to touch the hearts of

---

*This spiritual phenomenon is known as bilocation. Even while she dwelled upon the earth, tradition says that the Blessed Mother was able to be in more than one place at the same time when her presence was needed to fulfill God's Will for her as Mother of the Church.

the pagans of Saragossa with his promise that their lands would be a great and lasting center of Christianity. His courage-filled words were inspired by the Holy Spirit as he spoke in the name of the Son of the Queen of Angels. No one doubted. He brought truth to listeners with graced ears to hear.

A magnificent Baroque cathedral, known as Our Lady Del Pilar Sanctuary, was built at the site of the Queen of Angel's visit with James the apostle. Within the cathedral one can see and physically touch the actual jasper pillar upon which angels transported their Queen from Jerusalem to Saragossa two thousand years ago. The breathtaking beauty of the twelfth-century Portico de la Gloria lends encouragement to pilgrims to honor the age-old custom of making five personal prayer requests, at least three of which will be obtained from God by the Queen of Angels. Tens of thousands of pilgrims continue to flock to this holy place each month.*

---

*Santiago de Compostela was one of the most frequented places of pilgrimage from early Christendom. Pilgrims today find at Santiago much the same atmosphere that the cockleshell-wearing pilgrims found centuries ago. Preserved there for the use of pilgrims are the ancient stone streets of the old city that lead to many Romanesque churches and convents built in the Middle Ages, in addition to the great cathedral of Our Lady Del Pilar. Pilgrims embrace the ruby-encrusted thirteenth-century statue of Saint James and participate in an ancient incense ceremony of the swinging of the *Botafumeiro*. Legend is that the Apostle James appears to people in need of help, bringing miracles and consolation. Hence, he is acclaimed the patron saint of Spain.

According to local lore, after the martyrdom of Saint James in Jerusalem, angels transported his body to Santiago de Compostela for burial on the exact site where he once conferred with their Queen. Miracles have enriched untold millions of devout pilgrims during the last two thousand years.

A most dramatic healing was recorded on March 29, 1641. Nineteen-year-old pilgrim Michael Juan Pellicer, from Aragon, prayed fervently with great faith and determination to the Queen of Angels to intercede for him to recover his amputated leg. His prayer request was granted. His amputated leg, now throbbing with life and health and strength, was restored to him in an instant. Eye-witness testimony, records, and declarations of the miracle are dated March 12, 1642. They are signed by the surgeon who had made the amputation, the archbishop of Saragossa, the senior professor of canon law, and the vicar-general of the diocese. The records verifying the miracle have been preserved in Madrid at the College of the Society of Jesus. Cures and healing wrought through the intercession of the Queen of Angels continue all over the world, not just at Santiago de Compostela.

This book is arranged to show us all how to seek help from the Queen of Angels in many situations that trouble us in these times and all times. God's Plan is being realized in the world. We are each part of that Plan. The Queen of Angels energizes us to love as God would have us love. The more we love, the closer we are to God. The Queen of Angels is among us to explain to us how to be faithful to God's ways, how to be living peace. When we are aware of her presence, we never doubt, we never fear, we are able to love as God would have us love. When we truly love, we become living peace.

During a lecture at the IMF/World Bank prayer group in Washington, D.C., several years ago, a woman asked if she could speak to me privately. The London-trained Ph.D. in economics, who chairs a department, told me that she was experiencing the presence and guidance of Mary, Queen of Angels. The woman mentioned her professional goal to develop and augment better living conditions for the people of Africa. She insisted that with Mary's help, her prayer life had increased, and as her prayer life grew, so also did her wisdom.

It is the height of wisdom to welcome the Queen of Angels, to trust her love and protection in every circumstance of our lives. She will never fail us. She will never disappoint us. She appreciates and rewards the least little thing we do to please God. We are her beloved children. Jesus honors those who honor His Mother.

My former neighbor, of the Orthodox faith, escaped from behind enemy lines during World

War II. She was carrying a baby in her arms and held her three-year-old by the hand as she walked through mine fields to freedom. My neighbor promised the Queen of Angels that if she escaped unharmed with her children, and could find and be reunited with her husband, who was then a prisoner of war, she would fast strictly for world peace on Fridays for the rest of her life. She did escape, was later reunited with her husband, and lives a peaceful, prosperous, and virtuous life in the United States. She, of course, fasts strictly on Fridays and has also raised her children to do so.

During the Gulf War, Moslems and Christians flocked to the shrines of the Queen of Angels to pray and seek her protection for themselves and their loved ones.

We all do know the Queen of Angels in our hearts, and in deep prayer. We all seek to experience the joys and rewards of her presence as our Spiritual Mother Most Powerful, Most Loving, Most Faithful. May this book be a small instrument by which the Queen of Angels is better known and more widely loved throughout the world. It is my prayer that your prayer requests that she so generously carries to her Son on your behalf be quickly granted.

Prologue

LOOK AND DISCOVER
THE QUEEN OF ANGELS

Dear children of God,
I am Queen of Angels.

I am the lowly servant,
obedient messenger, and trained ambassador of
Our Father, my Son, and the Holy Spirit.

I am here now in a way that has never before been
granted to mankind.
I shall bless those children of God
who invite me into their hearts, their homes,
their decisions, their journey to God.
I am raising up a coterie of followers
whose faithfulness to God's will
is changing the earth.

Come into the safety of my Immaculate Heart,
dear little children.
Do not be dismayed by what unfolds around you.
Our Father is changing the direction
of your lives.
You shall know peace as you surrender
to His ways.
There are great rewards for those who surrender
to His ways.

My heart is filled with my Son, Jesus.
Turn to my motherly heart.
There you find the consolation you crave.
My heart is filled with Joy.
Share abundantly, dear children, in my Joy.
Seek to remain in my heart, dear children.
There, I give you my Son.
It is my Son who lifts you into the Empyrean
Valleys of Love.
Together, you climb to the Heights of Love.

It is Jesus who is Love.
Those who dwell with me
dwell on the Heights of God's Love and
Providence.
Love God's will as it unfolds around you.
Seek to please God alone.
Then you shall know great peace.

My words, in these times, are not a road map
to human aspirations.
I come to bring the Plan of our Father.
His Plan is Eternal Life for all His children.
Those who cling to human dreams do not find
the Path of Jesus.
Jesus alone is the Way, the Truth, and the Light
for your journey to Paradise.
Jesus is Humble.
Jesus is Pure.
Jesus is Wisdom.
Jesus is Compassion.
Jesus is Knowledge.
Jesus is Abundance.

Ponder the words of Jesus.
Jesus is God.
Jesus *will* rule all His Father's children.
Soon the hour arrives when the Good Shepherd
shall be recognized.
I am preparing His sheep to hear His Voice.
Those who hear His Voice discover the means to
see Him,
to follow Him,
to dwell with Him forever.

It is the time of the return of my Son.
My Son shall be recognized as the Lord of the
Angels.

My Son calls now to the Lost Sheep of the
House of Israel.
Many do not hear His Voice, for my Son
is humble.
My Son is Peace.
My Son is Graciousness.
My Son is God.

Trust me, little children.
I am the Mother of God.
I am Queen of Angels.
I am Mother of all our Father's children.
I am the Queen of the Earth, dear little children.
Each of you who draws near my heart
enters into the courtyard
of God's Great Plan for
His little children of the earth.
The apostles were the first children of God
to experience the joy of my Immaculate Heart.
As they drew near me,
they comprehended more and more the dignity
God intends for each of you.

Dear little children,
draw nearer to my Immaculate Heart.
I am your hope.
I am your joy.
There are flowers in God's Garden that He
wishes me to give
to you.

The flowers of God's Love fill your minds and
imaginations
with Truth.
Truth is the language of Love.
As you dine on Love,
your bodies heal of all the poison of non-love
that has sickened God's dear little children.

Please me, little children, by taking pleasure
in this time
God has given to you
to come to know me better.
Please me, little children, by perfect trust in
His Plan for your lives.
Please me, little children, by your joy
as you embrace God's Plan for your lives.

I am with you, little ones.*
Do not disappoint me by dwelling on the past.
Leave the past forever.
It has no power over you unless you invite it,
nourish it, and foolishly indulge in it.

---

*Mary's presence with us cannot be compared to God's presence in
us by sanctifying grace, by which we are made partakers of Divine
Life. Mary is not omnipresent. Rather, as Mother of God, Mary is
morally present to us and we to her as she cooperates with the Holy
Spirit in forming Jesus in our souls. As St. Louis de Montfort explains:
"Mary is present in our souls as the sun is present in a room by its light
and warmth, even though it is not there itself."

Lot's wife could not accept God's Will.
She was therefore consumed with sorrow.

Move on, my dear children.
Move forward with great trust in my presence
and courage to accept God's Plan for your lives.
There are days ahead that will fill your human
hearts with amazement.
Prepare now to help the millions of souls
who shall depend upon your faithfulness
to God's Will for you.

There are days ahead that require your utmost
obedience.
Practice listening for my voice.
Listen at each moment.
When you hear my voice, respond with great joy
and enthusiasm.
My little ones have heard my call to them
in the winds
and the fog and the rains that have swept the
lands of earth.
Soon my children will have a new climate that
will memorialize
my return to their conscious awareness.
I am the Eternal Mother.
I am your Mother of Obedience to God's Will.
I am the Mother of God and Mother of all His
dear little children.

The Hand of God is upon the earth.
The Heart of God is upon the earth.
The Love of God is upon the earth.
The Will of God returns to the hearts of
His children.
Peace is the will of God.
Peace is the gift of God.
Peace is the fruit of the earth.

God has given each of you tasks.
Each of you is endowed with gifts to accomplish
those tasks.
Jesus has shown you the way.
Those who pray too little cannot follow the path
of my Son.
He comes to you now to have an accounting
of your gifts.

Many weep and mourn and die because
so few pray.
So few hear my voice.
So few allow me to visit in their hearts, their
homes, their work, their goals, their dreams,
their longings.

Few allow me hospitality.
Few invite me into their lives.
Few listen to my voice.
Few obey God's Will once I communicate it
to them.

Those who follow the ways of the world
forget to listen for my voice
in their adulation and self-esteem.
My heart weeps for the sorrow my children
heap upon themselves.

Please listen for my voice.
I have much to tell you.
I am Queen of Angels.
I am the Mother of all God's children.
Allow me to carry you in my heart to
the Prince of Peace,
the Lord of Lords,
the Alpha and the Omega.

Peace, little children.
Only peace.

Introduction

You and I are of one family. We each play a uniquely significant role in God's Plan for the human race. Every one of us is filled with distinguished gifts from the Heart of God. We are divinely created spirits endowed with magnificent treasures. We are much more than our human body and our human relationships, although both are important for our growth and development while on the earth and thereafter.

We come from Heaven and are destined to return to Heaven. When memories of our true homeland stir in the depths of our souls, we desire to reach out to all creation with praise and gratitude. At such moments, the Mother of God seems quite close. And she is.

God lives in each of us. Mary, Queen of Angels, lives and loves in God. She is the first among divinized human beings (ST. ATHANASIUS). Mary is the prototype and should be our role model of God's Plan for each one of us. When we seek direction, all we need to do is look to Mary. She has information we desire. She will lead us to the Heart of God's love, Jesus.

Solutions for a Wonderful Life

When trouble persists, go to the feminine. God has made it so. Mary is a special part of God's Plan for the human race. She offers a spiritual path for everyone, of all faiths and backgrounds, to find a way to the wonderful life we all crave. Mary, Mother of the Lord Jesus, is our ever-present, ever-loving Spiritual Mother. She patiently awaits our awakening to the reality of her presence at our side. Wisest of all mothers, she is our Mother Most Faithful, Most Prudent, Most Powerful.

Mary, Queen of Angels, a feminine expression of God's infinite power and love, helps each one of us journey out of human degradation, poverty, despair, and death. Mary's gentle way to the Heart of God is paved with simplicity and steeped in the majesty of God's Presence in all that lives. To discover Mary, Queen of Angels and chosen by God as our Spiritual Mother, is to allow her to accompany us now into the silent sanctuary of the Heart of God.

Secrets of Heaven

Jesus illumined the Feminine Face of God by entering humanity through, with, and in His human Mother. He showed us that the road of spiritual simplicity leads us to Mary, Queen of Angels, who bears the secrets of Heaven and earth to share with God's people. Drawing upon her wisdom, knowledge, and counsel, we discover our unique, personal, loving way to Jesus. To become deeply aware of Mary's presence as Queen of Angels is to taste her love and enter with her into the Heart of her Son, the prince of peace, the Lord of the Cosmos, the Alpha and the Omega.

Jesus, Son of Mary, makes all things new. His Mother is no exception. She who is Mother of God and Queen of Angels is the new Eve. A clear mirror of God's Will, Mary, Queen of Angels, is transparent like the air. We can learn to recognize her presence and avail ourselves of her strength and wisdom.

Chosen to bring us God's Son, Mary continues in that role eternally. Everyone's Mother, Mary, Queen of Angels, *is* the Light-bearer who brings eternal life to humanity. To kneel before her is to kneel before the Light that flows through her to all God's creation. Never worship the Light-bearer—only the Light is worthy of worship, for the Light is God.

The Humble Know

God is Living Humility. The portal to life in God is guarded by the virtue of humility. Mary is totally conformed to God's image and likeness. Humble Mary is closest to God. She knows God best of all His creatures. Mohammed assured his followers that Mary ranks highest among women in Heaven, and yet she is the most humble of all God's creatures.

The humble know Mary. A humble soul, like Mary, is a soul who works but uses not. A humble soul replenishes the earth. A humble soul is a source of life. A humble soul is a soul through whom God the Father renews. A humble soul is one through whom Jesus makes all things new. Mary, Queen of Angels, guides those who approach her to Jesus, who is Living Humility. Only the humble live on in Jesus. Those blinded by pride never see or hear Mary, Queen of Angels. They never find Jesus.

Our Spiritual Mother Protects Us

God's divine Plan appoints Mary Queen of Angels and Spiritual Mother of the human race. God sustains Mary as Mother of Life. She protects life. She stands at the threshold of death to defend her own. Her love is zealous. Mary preserves and ennobles her own. Through her Son, Mary, Queen of Angels, sees all things. She guards her children. God has given Mary a harbor to protect souls consecrated to her. Though the winds and waves of spiritual warfare assail, they never swamp her family.

One of us in all things but sin, the Queen of Angels desires to nurture us into the divine life of her Son, for whom all things were made. As Queen of Angels, Mary illumines for us the mysterious healing power, majesty, and glory of the Resurrected Christ.

All creation is filled with sights and sounds of the sacred. Each personal decision we make bears eternal, cosmic effects. Our Spiritual Mother has intimate access to hidden chambers in the divine palace reserved for cherished family members. Jesus said: "In My Father's House there are many mansions and I go to prepare a place for you that where I am, you may be also." We can decide if we want to be at table with the King of Kings and

Lord of Lords. Who can bring us closer to the Lord than His Mother?

Reader's Guide

This book is divided into treasures of Light and Love for every human challenge. Much of the text is presented in the first person for spiritual intimacy, which leads to divine wisdom. Questions are addressed to Mary, Queen of Angels and Spiritual Mother of the human race. Answers are rich with grace and illumination. Listen carefully with your heart as you ponder the given answers. If you patiently surrender to the Holy Spirit of Love, you will receive what you seek. Sensitively respond to whatever images or ideas express themselves. Conclude with gracious receptivity as you read the *Prayer.* Generously allow God to be God and fill you with awareness of God's loving presence in you, around you, and always with you.

Though there are many ways to benefit from this book, the best is a personally adapted version of the following:

1. Spend at least five minutes a day with Mary. (Fifteen is a goal for which to strive.)
2. Find a quiet place for uninterrupted prayer and communion.

3. Begin by closing your eyes and breathing in God's love deeply. Then slowly exhale your gratitude. Speak these words: "Lord, I place myself in Your presence."

4. Let go of worries that plague your mind. Watch them float away by trusting that Mother Mary will guide you to solace and a solution.

5. Say a prayer to Mary (the Hail Mary or some other prayer of praise and protection for guidance).

6. Read the *Question* aloud and then read the *Answer*. Listen to the words and let them speak to your heart.

7. Read the *Meditation*. Then close your eyes and consider the words.

8. Carry the words in your heart throughout the day. Let these words take root within you so that they grow and fill you with confidence and the security that God's love does and will sustain you.

9. Look carefully at the *Daily Application* and consider in what way you can put it to personal use immediately. If at first reading the suggestions seem esoteric, do remember that we are all unique and need to find our own way to Jesus. Trust the Holy Spirit to guide you as you ponder your own personal daily application.

10. Say the *Prayer* with as much faith and trust as possible.
11. Open Sacred Scripture and read at least one verse. Then sit still for a few moments and await God.
12. Conclude by gently breathing in God's love and exhaling your gratitude.

Cherish Mary as Queen of Angels and your own personal Spiritual Mother. She brings God's choicest blessings. For example, in Chapter Two, choose the divine gift you desire to enrich your life and follow Mary's way to the Heart of God's Love. You will taste pure love in that process. Or turn to Chapters Three and Four and avail yourself of spiritual cures. Turn frequently every day to Part Two and find calmness, courage, strength, and wisdom in the Queen of Angel's ways to embrace opportunities and solve life's pressing personal challenges.

Use the Table of Contents to find Mary's secrets from Heaven for any situation you face. Cherish the path of Love offered in each spiritual *Meditation* and *Prayer*. Mary's wisdom, understanding, knowledge, and counsel fill our days and nights on earth with warmth and abundance. She brings us spiritual peace, heartfelt joy, and abiding love, for whoever finds Mary gains Jesus. Divine light surrounds Mary's ways and nourishes our spirits at each prayerful reading of these solutions.

Gently accept this graced opportunity every day and enter into aloneness with the Queen of Angels. Present with us in Jesus, Mary always responds when we call to her. Embrace Mary's ways to the Heart of God and discover the joy of true union with our Father, her Son, and the Holy Spirit.

No one else is called to walk your path or mine. No one hears God as you or I do. If we allow her, the Queen of Angels will gently awaken us to conscious awareness of the sacred presence of God in us and around us. With her, we are not afraid. She brings immense consolation to us, especially in moments when we may feel like God's lost or forgotten children. Her presence with us is a perfume that purifies the stench of pride and frees us from our cages of fear.

God calls to us in our depths: *"We are one, o my beloved children. We are one."*

The Queen of Angels is here to help us see and hear God with the eyes and ears of the heart. Heaven is now for those who know God in Spirit and Truth.

Part One

LOOKING FOR PARADISE

AND I SAW A NEW HEAVEN AND A NEW
EARTH. FOR THE FIRST HEAVEN AND
THE FIRST EARTH WAS GONE, AND THE
SEA IS NOW NO MORE.

•

—*Revelation 21:1*

Peace Prayer for the Millennium

If you take me to the Source of Peace
O Mother of the Word Made Flesh,
I shall ask for glorious things for each of us.
Are we not God's precious flesh and blood?

Jesus, my Source of Peace,
if You send me to the highways and byways
of the earth,
I shall awaken your faithful children.
I shall help your faithful children.
We will serve our Father with gratitude
and enthusiasm.

Jesus, my Source of Peace,
we shall end racial bigotry, for You are
our Good Shepherd,
we are Your flock.

Jesus, my Source of Peace,
we shall end ethnic bigotry, for You are

the Vine,
We are Your branches.

Jesus, my Source of Peace,
we shall end gender bias, for You are
Son of God,
we are Your family.

Jesus, my Source of Peace,
we shall eliminate poverty, for You are
Lord of all Creation,
we are Your creatures.

Jesus, my Source of Peace,
we shall eliminate disease, for You are
Lover of the Sick,
we are Your own.

Jesus, my Source of Peace,
we shall eliminate hatred that begets violence,
for You are Living Peace,
we are Your brother, sister, mother.

O Creator,
we shall create from Your earth
breath-taking beauty carved out of love for You.

O Unending Love,
we shall use our talents and gifts to magnify
the Presence of Your Love in each of us.

Reign, O Source of Peace, for You are
Life.

Come Queen of Angels,
Mary, my Spiritual Mother.
You alone are Mother of the Lord of all.
You alone are Queen of Heaven and Queen
of God's vast creation.

Come, Queen of Angels,
my own Spiritual Mother.
Show me secrets from Serene Sanctuaries
in the depths of Divinity
hidden in Jesus' Divine Heart of Love.

Mother of God,
Mother of me and mine,
when the Source of Peace arises on the dawn of
hope, surely in God's great world of love and truth,
no sorrows will remain in us.

Beginning of No Beginning,
You are making all things new
in countless little miracles
that I shall ask to see
when the Source of Peace
arrives in Chariot of Flaming Clouds.

Hope against all hopes, my heart.
The angels sound their horns

and nature glistens with tears
that quickly wash away my fears.

"I Am Who Am," He calls.
God's Power, God's Love,
God's Providence resound
in all that is
and was
and is to be.

Be still.
The Prince of Peace draws near.
The Queen of Angels is here.
Listen with your heart and you shall hear.

Chapter One

TREASURES

*When Jesus saw his mother and the disciple there whom he
loved, he said to his mother, "Woman behold your son."
Then he said to the disciple, "Behold your mother." And
from that hour the disciple took her into his home.*
—John 19:26–27

The Gift of Mary

*Jesus, if the desire of loving You is so delightful,
what will it be to possess and enjoy this Love?*
—St. Therese of Lisieux

Love is repaid by love alone.
—St. John of the Cross

Q. WHO ARE YOU, MARY?
A. I am the eternal Mother of Jesus. I am your Spir-

itual Mother. I am the parting gift my Son Jesus gave
to the human race before His death on the cross.

Q. BLESSED MOTHER, WHO IS JESUS?
A. Jesus is the Lord. He alone is the Lord. He is
the Ruler. He is the Son of the Father and son of
me. Jesus is the Word made flesh. Jesus is your
Brother.

Q. IS JESUS THE BROTHER OF EVERY HUMAN BEING?
A. Yes, my child.

Q. WHY DOESN'T EVERYONE KNOW JESUS IF HE IS
OUR BROTHER?
A. God speaks in many different ways to His
people of the earth. Those who hear His voice
and respond to His invitations come to God
quickly. God invites everyone into His Kingdom
of Love (JOHN 14:15–21). God's people encounter Jesus in God's time and in God's way.

Meditation

Jesus gave His Mother to me. Mary, my Spiritual Mother, loves me unconditionally, individu-
ally, just as I am. Mary is my own Mother most
Powerful. Her power is rooted in God's love for
her and for me. Am I totally comfortable with my
Spiritual Mother given to me by the Son of God?
God does tell me, in millions of ways, of His di-

vine providence caring for each of us, at all times, as we are, as we were, and as we will be. Am I listening? God promises that those who seek Him find Him. God is life-giving light.

Daily Application

Today I say hello to my Spiritual Mother. Today I look for evidence of her presence as Spiritual Mother in my life. Today I ask her to lead me closer to awareness of God's presence in me and around me.

Prayer

Hail Mary, full of grace, the Lord is with you. Blessed are you among women, and blessed is the fruit of your womb, Jesus. Holy Mary, Mother of God, pray for us sinners now, and at the hour of our death. Amen.

Humanity's Eternal Destiny

The Immaculate Virgin, preserved from all stain of original sin, was taken up, body and soul into heavenly glory, when her earthly life was over, and exalted by the Lord as Queen over all things, that

she might be the more fully conformed to her Son,
the Lord of Lords, and conqueror of sin and death.
—*Second Vatican Council*

Q. BLESSED MOTHER, ARE YOU A SPIRIT?
A. Yes, my child.

Q. DO YOU HAVE A BODY, BLESSED MOTHER?
A. Yes, my child. It is spiritualized.

Q. BLESSED MOTHER, WILL MY BODY BE SPIRITUAL-
IZED TOO?
A. That gift of God our Father is reserved for
all those who remain faithful to His Plan for them
(1 CORINTHIANS 42–44). The resurrection of
the body is a mercy of God whereby His children's
corporeal substance is restored to its intended
splendor.

Meditation

Mary, my Spiritual Mother, loves me unconditionally. She will never abandon me: She wants
to help me. My body houses my spirit that lives
forever. My body will be spiritualized in a wonderful way if I remain faithful to God's Plan for
me. Mary is aware of God's perfect Plan for me.
Her guidance can help me follow God's perfect
Plan for me so that I may experience Heaven even

now with God and all His angels and saints. I have decisions to make that beget eternal consequences.

Daily Application

Today, I recognize the eternal destiny of my indwelling spirit. I will think about my eternal destiny when my body requires anything of me, especially when I am hungry or thirsty.

Prayer

Mary, my spiritual Mother, we have been taught: "Your stainless body did not remain within the earth; you were transported alive to the royal abode of Heaven; you who are at once Queen and Sovereign, and very truly the Mother of God. How could you taste death who has given Life to all?" (ST. JOHN DAMASCENE).

Holy Mary, Mother of God, pray for me that I may realize and be actualized in the promises of your Son, the Resurrected Christ. Amen.

QUEEN OF OUR FATHER'S HEART

*Who can conceive how great is the glory of the
Queen of the world? As she advanced [to
Heaven], with what depth of devotion and
affection the angels and saints, the whole
multitude of heavenly citizens, went forth to
welcome her. With what magnificent canticles she
was conducted to her glorious throne; with what
gracious bearing, serenity of countenance. Her Son
received her with divine embraces and exalted her
above all creatures, with the honor His Mother
merited. She was crowned with the glory that
reflects her majestic Son.*
—St. Bernard of Clairvaux

Q. BLESSED MOTHER, ARE YOU A QUEEN?
A. Few understand my Queenship. I am not a
Queen as the world understands the title. I am
Spiritual Mother of all our Father's children. I
give my children His Heart that they may taste
His love. Soon all God's children shall recognize
their Mother. When they know their own
Mother, they shall have their identity. When God's
children know who they are, their hearts will melt
into mine. Together we shall dwell before the
Trinity, for holy is His Name and holy are His
ways. We are one, dear little children, in my Immaculate Heart.

Q. BLESSED MOTHER, ARE YOU MY QUEEN?

A. I am the Queen of Heaven and Earth. I am the Daughter of our Father. I am the Mother of His Only Begotten Son. I am Mother of all the children of our Father.

I am Queen of Angels. Their mission is to protect my children. Their ways are obvious to those who know me well. Peace, dearest child. Rest in my heart. Accept my protection.

Meditation

God desires me to be happy, to be contented in this life and forever. God desires me to allow the Queen of Angels to help me live God's perfect Plan for me, minute by minute and day by day. She understands God's Will for me. She has special grace just for me. Will I truly allow my Spiritual Mother to mother me? Will I accept her sweet spiritual milk? Will I allow her to bring me God's peace? Will I allow her to carry me into God's divine life? Jesus Christ has overcome the darkness. Will I allow His Mother to carry me to Him who is Light from Light?

Daily Application

Today I desire to be one with God (JOHN 14:7–11). Today I choose God's ways by thinking about my immortal soul before I speak and act. Today I choose to read Sacred Scripture. Today, I choose to emulate Jesus' life, His relationship with God our Father. Today I seek awareness of the Holy Spirit by disciplining myself to embrace active silence. Today I await knowledge of God's presence, power, and divine life. Today, I allow Jesus to send the Holy Spirit of Love to awaken me to God's eternal presence, eternal love, and immutable truth.

Prayer

Holy Mary, Mother of God, Queen of Creation, Queen of my heart, Queen of Angels, your Son Jesus is God from God. I desire to recognize Him, to know Him, to love Him, to learn from Him, to obey Him, to lean on Him, to rest upon His Heart. Help me to allow Jesus, the source of peace, to reign forever in my heart, mind, and soul.

The Way of Knowledge

Mary is full indeed of grace, full of God, full of virtues, she could not but possess most fully the glory of eternal splendor.
—St. Jerome

Q. BLESSED MOTHER, DO YOU KNOW ME?
A. Yes, my child. I know everything about you. I love you. You are my gift and I am your gift.

Q. BLESSED MOTHER, HOW AND WHY DO YOU KNOW ME?
A. I know you in Jesus, with Jesus, for Jesus. My Son Jesus has given you to me. My Son Jesus has given me to you. Be at peace in the life God has given us. There is no suffering you experience that I do not experience also. What I will give you is better than anything you will keep for yourself.

Meditation

Mary knows everything about me because God has so ordained from all eternity. Mary knows God as no other human. Mary is the eternal splendor of God's divine Love. Mary desires to help me truly know God now. Mary has power and wisdom and grace from God to bring solutions to all my difficulties. Will I allow Mary to help me now? God's presence and power are everywhere. Do I experience their effects every day? Mary helps me enter into conscious awareness of God's presence and power all around me.

Daily Application

Do I recognize God's hand in the sweet chirping of His birds? From now on I remember who created the birds. I remember the One whom their song glorifies. From now on I see God's handiwork in His trees, His flowers, His people, His earth, His planets, and all creation. The time to see God and hear God is now. From now on, when I experience difficulties, I remember we are all born in the "land of exile," a miserable state of being in which we do not know and we do not experience eternal, unconditional love (GENESIS 1). Today I remember that God calls us immediately out of misery to walk with Him in His Kingdom of Love (GENESIS 3:15). The journey need not be long. Today, I desire to hear God's voice, to know God's presence, to respond to His invitations. Today, I desire to run quickly to God, forever.

Prayer

Great God of Love, I run to you now in my heart, my mind, my will, my soul, and my spirit. Draw me ever nearer to You until I truly know we are one. Allow me to recognize the help You provide to make my journey to Your waiting arms a blessing of peace, joy, and love. Thank You, dear God, for the gift of Mary, Queen of Angels. May her presence with me remain, by my choices, a sign of Your great love for me and my great love for You, forever. Amen.

The Presence of Eternal Splendor

God showed me in part the wisdom and the truth
of [Mary's] soul: wherein I understood the reverent
beholding in which she beheld her God and
Maker, marveling with great reverence that He
would be born of her that was a simple creature of
His making. And this wisdom and truth—knowing
the greatness of her Maker and the littleness
of herself that was made—caused her to
say full meekly to [the Archangel] Gabriel:
"Lo, me, God's handmaid!" In this sight
I understood truly that she is more than all
that God made beneath her in worthiness
and grace, for above her is nothing that is made
but the blessed Manhood of Christ. . . .
—*Blessed Dame Julian of Norwich*

Q. BLESSED MOTHER, THE MYSTERIES OF JESUS, OF YOU, OF THINGS OF GOD ARE DIFFICULT TO GRASP. CAN YOU HELP ME UNDERSTAND?
A. When you ponder too deeply the mystery of God made man in Jesus Christ with only your

intellect, you assail God's unfathomable Love for
you. Recognize God's unconditional Love for
you. Accept God's Love. Allow God to embrace
you in divine Love. Love. Love. Only Love. Experience my presence in your life. Allow me to love
you. I greatly desire to bring you to my Son Jesus.
Allow me to prepare your heart to receive Him.
Love. Love always my child. Love in deed and
Truth.

Meditation

God is Spirit and Truth. I can only know God
in Spirit and Truth. I cannot find God with my
mind. It is a labyrinth with many avenues of deception. To love God, obey God, remain faithful
to God, is to know God. God is the Way and the
Truth and the Light. God is life. God loves me.
God's Love is power. God is calling me. It is far
more benign to seek God than to force God to
seek me. Our Father is a jealous God who toler-
ates no idols, or idolatrous ways (JOHN 15:4–6). I
desire to find the gentle way, steeped in simplicity,
to look for God. Do I and will I accept Mary's
way?

Daily Application

I find time, when I see the trees, to sit and wait
for God. Today, I see God's hand in nature. I feel

the warmth of God's sun. Today, silence is my prayer as I await God. I say nothing. Think nothing. Just wait. God comes to me when I least expect. God alone brings the joy and peace and delight I seek (JOHN 14:6).

Prayer

Mary, help me to hear your gentle, loving voice. Carry me in your arms to God as you carried Jesus. Be with me consciously in my times of unknowing. Turn every dark moment into treasures of trust in God who is the resurrection of all my dreams and longings. Sing to me of God's Love in the sweet melodies of your constant, affirming, loving presence. Help me transcend the limits of space and time now and dwell consciously with God forever. Amen.

THE REALITY OF UNCONDITIONAL LOVE

*I always find a way of being happy and of
profiting from my miseries.*
—*St. Therese of Lisieux*

Q. BLESSED MOTHER, IS IT POSSIBLE FOR US TO TRULY
LOVE ONE ANOTHER UNCONDITIONALLY?

A. Only those who pray learn how to truly love.
Read the words of Jesus every day. Learn the
words of Jesus. Follow the path of Jesus. Live the
life Jesus showed you. Remember the nights that
Jesus spent in prayer. Exercise. Walk outside. Only
eat what is good for your body. When your mind
and body are in harmony, obedient to God's perfect Plan for you, your spirit becomes free to soar
to the heights of Love. Jesus promised that when
two people join voices on earth to pray in His
Name for anything whatsoever, thus shall it be
granted. When you walk, work, exercise, rest, experience my presence. Praise Jesus with me at
every moment. Know that I walk, work, exercise,
live, rest, sing, minister, and die with you while
praying for you to love with you eternally. Join
your heart to mine now, dear child of my Immaculate Heart. Pray with me always, for when we

join voices on earth to pray in Jesus' Name for anything whatsoever, thus shall it be granted.

Meditation

Mary, Queen of Angels is here with me now. She understands and obeys God's Will perfectly. She trusts God's perfect Will, even at the foot of the cross as her innocent Sacred Son dies in contempt. Sara, the wife of Abraham, was God's obedient, though unenlightened, daughter. Sara struggled in pain and sorrow to find and obey God's Will. Like Sara, I repeatedly fail to trust God's words to Abraham (GENESIS 15:1–6; 22:16–18). Dissonance, confusion, and pain flow from my doubts. Mary trusts perfectly the Covenant God made with Abraham and his seed forever. Every human on the earth is a blood-bought child of the Covenant God made with Abraham. God is the Faithful One. God's love is unconditional. I must learn to love as God loves.

Daily Application

Today, I trust God's promises. Today, I trust Mary's power to understand God's perfect Will and graciously communicate that Plan to me. Today, with her help, I shall be faithful to God's ways, minute by minute and second by second. Today, I remind myself I am a blood-bought child of the Covenant God has made with His people. I am a pearl of great price ransomed by the Blood of the Lamb. Today I behave for God who is the Faithful One. Today, God offers me His life, His ways, His Heart. Today, I begin, or continue on with, my daily journal (a personal spiritual diary).* Today, I consciously choose God's life, God's ways. Today, I seek God's perfect Plan for my life.

Prayer

Queen of Angels, did you teach Jesus to pray? Or did He teach you to pray before He made the world? Pray to God with me as you prayed with Jesus when He too walked the earth as I do now. I desire to know Jesus truly as He is. Please ask Jesus to reveal to me secrets of the Sacred Scriptures in

---

*Every day, without fail, record in a private spiritual diary your experiences, needs, sorrows, joys, and desires. By carefully tracking your personal journey to God, you may observe and speed up your spiritual growth and development. Over time, this spiritual journal will prove an invaluable resource that allows you to overcome many hidden obstacles that sabotage your peace, confidence, and personal growth and development. The simplest spiritual diary includes the following information: 1) How you feel that day 2) Why you feel that way (it is all right not to know why you feel a certain way, but do note that too) 3) Who and what you have encountered during the day and their effects on you 4) An honest evaluation of how, where, and why God does or does not fit into your day and your experiences 5) A small personal prayer for Light. (Some samples of a day in a spiritual journal are contained in the Appendix.)

the Light of the Holy Spirit of Love. Please help me to fast with joy and peace, to recognize and run from occasions that lead me to peril, to avoid things and people and places that obscure the Kingdom of Heaven all around us. Let me always know and obey God's Will in everything, to trust God totally. Please ask God to fill me now with divine peace. Queen of Angels, pray that I love only God's ways.

ACCEPTING GOD'S GOOD GIFT

[Holy Mary is] Queen of the world, Queen of Heaven. . . . the tabernacle of God. . . . the celestial ladder by which the King of Heaven descended to earth, and man ascends to Heaven.
—*St. Peter Damian*

Q. BLESSED MOTHER, HOW LONG HAVE YOU KNOWN ME?
A. I know you from the beginning. I love you immeasurably. Do not speak of my secrets to you with anyone. Rest in my love. Treasure our relationship. It is God's gift to us.

Meditation

Mary, my Spiritual Mother, is God's good gift to me during this lifetime on earth and forever in Heaven. She is present in my life. She knows God better than I. She lives in Heaven, yet she is here with me constantly. Do I see my Spiritual Mother in my mind's eye? Do I consciously allow her to pray with me? God is making all things new in countless mornings of resurrection.

Daily Application

Today, I recognize my Spiritual Mother here with me praying for me each moment. I place her image where it will remind me that wherever Mary is, so also is Jesus. Today, I pray to grow in love and wisdom and knowledge. Today, I guard carefully my interior prayer-life with Mary, for she illumines the Kingdom of God for me in ways I most deeply need.

Prayer

Dear God, my Father, thank You for creating me, thank You for all life, thank You for this special time with my Spiritual Mother, this good gift to me. In Jesus' Name, I ask to grow in wisdom, knowledge, and love. Fill me with the power of the Holy Spirit of Love. Grant me strength to follow Mary's advice, to embrace her wisdom and trust Your divine Plan just for me. Renew my heart with powerful sweetness of Your healing Love. Nurture all that lives in the cauldron of Your Will. Thank You, Jesus, Only Begotten Son of the Eternal Father for the good gift of Your Mother. Jesus, Lamb of God, take away the sins of the world now. Jesus, Lord of mercy, restore my innocence. Like King David before the Ark of the Covenant, may I walk with God, dance and rejoice in God's presence, take delight in God's providence, relax in God's protection, pray with God's happiness, sing and frolic in God's great goodness, graciousness, and abiding kindness.

Chapter Two

HEIGHTS OF LOVE

The Presence of God is comprehensible only in the Light of the Holy Spirit of Love. Mary is the Spouse of the Holy Spirit of Love.
—St. Maximilian Kolbe

Power for Today

So he said to Samuel, "Go to sleep, and if you are called, reply 'Speak Lord, for your servant is listening.'" When Samuel went to sleep in his place, the Lord came and revealed his presence, calling out as before, "Samuel, Samuel!" Samuel answered, "Speak, for your servant is listening."
—1 Samuel 3:9

Q. BLESSED MOTHER, WHAT DO YOU WANT OF ME TODAY?

A. Focus today only on today's duties. Do not think of tomorrow. If today you hear His voice, harden not your heart. Prepare yourself, dear child, to receive the Lord Your God. Do not eat foolish things. Please exercise more. Give your family to me. They are better off with me. I will never abandon you.

Meditation

I brought nothing into this world, nor shall I take anything with me when I must depart the earth. Only my spirit lives forever. My spirit and I are one. Love begets Love. Hatred begets hatred. Which do I choose?

Daily Application

Today, I will carefully observe my habits and pray for the Light to embrace more spiritually enriching activities while discarding everything that draws darkness upon me.

Prayer

Spiritual Mother, I gladly give you my family, especially my body. Teach me to guard my body, this temple in which I must dwell while I trod the paths of this earth. Spiritual Mother, Mother of Divine Wisdom, explain to me the mysteries of the earth. How shall I work today? How shall I dine today? How shall I exercise today? How shall I preserve relationships I treasure? How shall I accomplish the dreams and longings that fill my mind and body? Impart your wisdom to me. Thank you for taking care of me. I have not yet developed eyes and ears that know Truth. If today you hear His voice calling to me, please ask God to call and call until I hear and respond, "Speak Lord. Your servant listens."

Power Over Fear

Arise, my beloved, my beautiful one, and come!
For see, the winter is past, the rains are over and
gone. The flowers appear on the earth, the
time of pruning the vines has come, and the
song of the dove is heard in our land.
—*Song of Songs 2:10–12*

Q. BLESSED MOTHER, DO YOU SEE EVERYTHING I DO?
A. I do. Live in order. Live in cleanliness. I will take care of you. Trust me. I love you totally. My love is power. Turn to me when you struggle. Rely on my power. I am the Mother of God. I am your Spiritual Mother. You are never alone. Do not be afraid.

Meditation

My Spiritual Mother is Mother of God, who has endowed her with sublime dignity. Her dignity is mine if I am faithful to God's perfect Will for me. I cannot yet comprehend the depths of God's Plan for me. My Spiritual Mother's biological son is Jesus, who is the Lord God, my Brother. The Mother of my Lord is my own Spiritual Mother. When I allow these truths to be my life, I recognize that God is with me and none can be against me.

Daily Application

Today, I pray for the divine gift of a grateful heart.

Today, I look for God's blessings hidden everywhere.

Today, I trust God loves me into being, sustains me, cares for my every need the best way for me.

Today, I hand every fear to Jesus.

Today, I trust Jesus, who loves me unconditionally.

Today, I allow God to solve my problems.

Prayer

Spiritual Mother, thank you for being here with me, for praying for me and with me always, for loving with me, for taking care of people and things and places I love, for treasuring in me what is decent and good and holy, for protecting me from what is not. Please give Jesus all my needs and desires. Ask Him to free me from my cage of fear. Ask Him to bring me to the mountain of peace. Please give me peace.

Power Over Suffering

You would have no power over me if it had not been given to you from above.
—John 19:11

Q. DEAR SPIRITUAL MOTHER, WHY IS THERE SUFFERING, OF EVERY KIND, IN OUR LIVES?
A. Dear child of my heart, you learn from experience, and every experience you have contributes to your character. Consider how your recovery from each misfortune contributes to your own personal interior strength and serves as an example to others. Pray during all suffering. Your prayers are an offering of yourself and your sufferings to God. This gift is a jewel without price.

Q. WHAT IS THE BEST WAY TO ENDURE SUFFERING I CANNOT AVOID?
A. When you drink deep of the cup of suffering, be consoled with the knowledge that I am near to you in your sorrow and tribulation. No harm shall befall you. Ponder the mystery of my Son's crucifixion and subsequent resurrection. Our Father chastises those He loves.

Q. WHY, DEAR BLESSED MOTHER?
A. Chastisement purifies the human heart and prepares it to receive God in fullness. Do not become bitter. Do not enter into the sorrows of those who refuse to carry their crosses in peace and obedience to the ways of my Son Jesus. No life on earth is free of the cross. Those who love our Father carry their crosses in peace and graciousness.

Q. HOW DO I CARRY MY OWN CROSS—SUFFER IN PEACE AND GRACIOUSNESS?
A. Entrust your woes to my Immaculate Heart. There you find peace, for there you encounter my Son Jesus in deepest intimacy.

Q. HOW CAN I HELP OTHERS WHO SUFFER?
A. Pray for those who suffer and for their families. Many languish in toil and sorrow, for their path is strewn with obstacles they observe not. As they submit to the hand of God, their fears shall melt in the caldron of God's Will.

Q. HOW CAN I OVERCOME MY FEAR OF SUFFERING?
A. Do not fear difficulties if they flow from the hand of our Father. Your path is obedience steeped in love. Rest in the confidence of my protection and my presence. Do not fear. Pray more, little one. Rest in my Heart of Love. I am the Mother of Life in God.

Meditation

We all encounter personal suffering in this life. When we suffer in prayer, we endure and we are strong. When we suffer without prayer, we complain and we are weak. Sufferings offered to God become my priceless gems in the heavenly Kingdom.

Daily Application

Today, I ponder the real source of my suffering. Nothing happens to me that God does not allow. Though I do not like suffering, it is an opportunity for interior greatness and spiritual wealth.

Prayer

Dear God, today, I offer to you all the suffering I experience, in union with the sufferings of Jesus. May Your Light and goodness mollify the pain in my being, soothe the sorrow in my heart, and lift the darkness from my mind and weakness from my will. Amen.

Power Over Death

[S]uffering alone gives birth to souls.
—St. Therese of Lisieux

Q. SPIRITUAL MOTHER, SHOULD I FEAR DEATH?
A. Jesus told us we are spirit and light. The body must be shed. This happens to everyone: some by war, by illness, by fatal accident. Some deaths are painless and quite peaceful. Dying is birth into a new form of life in God. Death is only the shedding of the human body. Though He died, Jesus lives. Though the saints died, they live. Our time on the earth is to develop our spirits that live forever.

Meditation

The cross of Jesus has given me royal blood. Jesus died that I may live forever. My Brother Jesus has saved me from eternal death.

Daily Application

I shall live forever in the Spirit. Each choice I make, while I inhabit my body on this earth, has eternal consequences for me. None of the dead in my family is gone. All are alive, in the Spirit, somewhere. Today, I thank God for the good things that have come to me through their sacrifices, and I pray for my family, each one from the beginning. Perhaps some of them are praying for me. I pray to make enlightened decisions that bear better eternal consequences for me and those I love.

Prayer

Thank you, Jesus. Thank you, Spiritual Mother. I fear nothing when I am with You. Please open my heart and intellect and fill me with awareness of Your eternal presence here with me. Dear God, Your Love for me is incomprehensible. Help me to make enlightened decisions at every moment—decisions that bear sweet, eternal fruit I can never lose. Help me always to remember that my life is not just a moment but lasts forever. Remind me always that my spirit is eternal. While I am in my body, help me make choices that yield positive consequences for me and my loved ones, forever. Please guard my every thought, word, and deed. You give me Your own Mother to share sublime treasures of Your providential Love. Dear God, please help me to respond with my whole heart, mind, and will so that I do not even notice the passing from this life form to the next.

Power for Families

Beware of false prophets, who come to you in sheep's clothing, but underneath are ravenous wolves. By their fruits you will know them.
—*Matthew 7:15–16*

Q. Blessed Mother, what about my family?
A. Your family must come first in your choices. Your family belongs to me. Serve your family and you serve me. My Son served His Father.

Q. Blessed Mother, will you please help me to understand my family so that I may be more faithful and more loving?
A. When you love your family and serve your family, you love and serve God. If you understand that truth, you are steeped in wisdom. Make your home orderly. Make your home peaceful. Consecrate your home to God. Allow God to dwell in your home. Then you will dwell in God. God is Humility. God does not come where He is not

honored. Welcome God with love. Those who love and serve God experience God's divine joy. Divine joy falls abundantly upon those who dwell near Him. As you love and serve your family in the home you have consecrated to God, consciously experience my presence with you. Soon, you will notice that where I am, so also is Jesus.

Meditation

I need the gift of wisdom to understand God's ways. God is present in all that lives. I long to see God, to hear God. The presence of God alone leads me to the Promised Land. Mary presents me the presence of God in corporeal form.

Daily Application

Today, I surrender all my relationships to my Spiritual Mother. She knows how to harmonize my relationships in the light of God's Love. Today, I practice silence so that my spiritual ears may hear.

Prayer

O Lord, You have given everything its place, in my family in the world, in the vast galaxies, and no one can make it otherwise. Everything is Your creation, the heavens and the earth and the stars:

people and animals and trees and plants and fishes. You are the Lord of all. You alone are God. Help me to recognize the gifts and wonders and treasures You so bountifully have placed in my family. Please impart great mercy to all my family, living, deceased, and yet to be born. Grant that each of us may truly love You. Allow us to taste Mary's motherly kindness flowing forth to all creation as she suffered with You at the cross for all of us. Help everyone in my family to use Your Blessed Mother's strength as You taught us by doing so Yourself. You who are the Lord of Hosts has placed each of us in our family. May we desire only to grow in wisdom, in love, and faithfulness to Your perfect Plan forever. May we truly love one another as You would have us love. Amen.

Power to Forgive

Do to others, whatever you would have them do
to you. This is the law and the prophets.
—*Matthew 7:12*

Q. SPIRITUAL MOTHER, HOW DO I STAY FOCUSED ON TODAY AND EXPERIENCE ABIDING PEACE, JOY, AND LOVE WHEN I ENCOUNTER PAINFUL, DESTRUCTIVE THOUGHTS OR ACTIONS OR PEOPLE? MY WOUNDS ARE DEEP.

A. Live each moment steeped in my love. Be confident of my love. Pray more fervently for wisdom. Always choose wisely. To be like Jesus you must forgive. If you are not like Jesus, you will not be able to find Him to choose Him. Help all your brothers and sisters to be like Jesus by your example. Pray. In prayer, you receive the power to forgive. Persevere in prayer. Treasure these moments we share each day. Jesus is always here for you. Turn to Jesus now. Turn to Jesus always. Never look away, even for a moment. Kneel in your mind before the Pietà: see how I forgave those who killed my Son. Pray more to obtain my help. Seek forgiveness in all your failings. God never withholds forgiveness to those who seek. God's perfect Will must be your will in all things. Never consciously rebel against God's Will in anything. Give any lack of forgiveness to Jesus now. Trust His divinity. Jesus is the Divine Physician sent to heal the pain and sickness of sin and death. Give all your burdens to Jesus now. Entrust your wounds to His sacred hands. If today you hear His voice, harden not your heart. Pray my child. Love. Only love.

Meditation

God is. God made me. God calls to me constantly in the depths of my longings. God loves me in all circumstances. God alone can make me perfect. My weakness is God's power. Only when I surrender to God's ways does His power overcome my inadequacies. To withhold forgiveness is to give my enemies power over me. I shall befriend my enemies; in that way, they shall have no power over me. I choose now to surrender to the power of God's Love. I forgive and forgive and forgive. In God alone is my salvation.

Daily Application

Who has wounded me the most? Today, I hand over _____ to Jesus.

Who has offended my integrity? Today, I hand over _____ to Jesus.

Who has deprived me of dignity or property or relationship or love? Today, I hand over _____ to Jesus.

Prayer

Spiritual Mother, kindly pray with me to Jesus now. Ask His special blessing upon my thoughts, words, and deeds, my days and nights, my yesterdays and tomorrows. Please ask Jesus to change my heart into living peace, abiding joy, and total love for all God's creation forever.

POWER TO BE BEAUTIFUL

*[Beauty] is more precious than corals, and none of
your choice possessions can compare with her. Her
ways are pleasant ways, and all her paths are
peace. She is a tree of life to those who grasp her,
and he is happy who holds her fast.*
—Proverbs 3:15, 17–18

Q. SPIRITUAL MOTHER, WHY ARE YOU SO BEAUTIFUL?
A. God alone is beauty. You become what you
observe. I am beautiful because I always look at
God. If you want to be beautiful, look always to
God. Prayer opens your eyes and ears to the living
presence of God whose Name is Love. Keep your
eyes only on the glories of God's Love all around
you. Listen only for His voice throughout creation. Pray with me now. Pray always in my love.

Meditation

The Apostle Peter took his eyes from Jesus and
sank into the stormy sea. So it is with me. When I
forget to pray, my eyes fall away from God's unconditional Love. Peter cried out to the Lord in his
terror. Jesus rescued him from the stormy depths.
Peter kept his eyes on God, even as he was crucified upside down for his belief in Mary's Son.

Daily Application

From now on, I consciously avoid what is not beautiful, peaceful, salubrious, and uplifting. Anything less, I immediately give to Jesus to renew and sanctify all that is not well.

Prayer

Dear God, please help me to keep my eyes on Your Kingdom of Love and goodness forever. Give me courage to embrace silence, to listen with love and acceptance to the sounds of the sacred spirit world. You alone are living beauty. Enter into me and abide with me forever.

Power to Be God's Prayer

The Holy Spirit shall come upon you.
—Luke 1:35

Mary is called the temple of the Lord and the sacred resting-place of the Holy Spirit: for by the operation of the Holy Spirit she became the Mother of the Incarnate Word.
—St. Thomas Aquinas

Q. SPIRITUAL MOTHER, WILL YOU SHOW ME GOD'S
WAYS? WILL YOU TEACH ME TO PRAY? FOR YOU KNOW
THE WAY.

A. Consciously experience my presence at all times.
I want you to know my Son, Jesus. Stay near me. Always obey God, who is your Father. Rest now in my
love as I speak to you of prayer. Prayer is the Bread
of Life. Jesus is the Bread of Life. All else is deception. All else is death. I am Queen of Peace. I am
Mother of God. I am Mother of humanity. I am living prayer. Through prayer, humanity knows peace.
Through peace, humanity experiences God. The
path to God is prayer. The path to God is Jesus. Jesus is Life. Jesus is Living Peace. Through Jesus you
experience God. Your life is God's prayer. How do
you respond to God's prayer?

Meditation

My Spiritual Mother explains that I must pray
much to surrender totally to God's perfect, beautiful Plan for my life. Jesus showed us by example
to pray before and during each decision we make.
Our life choices stem from our will. My will is
weak and darkened when I do not pray. I cannot
discern God's beautiful Plan for me unless I pray
much. I desire the abundant life promised by Jesus.
Only in God's Will do I have eternal life. Without
prayer, I forfeit the good life. I choose the good
life. I will pray today as if my life depends upon it.

Daily Application

Today, I recognize that Heaven is for those who know God. My prayer links me with Eternal Energy.* Today, I imitate Jesus who fled to the mountain-tops to pray to our Father. Today, I commit myself to deep prayer. Today, I invest prayer in the governance of my life. I pray with all my heart for union with God's Will. In God, there is no yesterday or tomorrow. All is the eternal now. Through prayer, I awaken to my presence in the eternal now.

Prayer

My Spiritual Mother, please remain in my conscious awareness always. Inspire me when I am weak, gently speak to me when I am stressed, sing me lullabies of the wonders of God's Providence when I fall into fear, graciously cover me in the warmth of Jesus' divine love for you and for me forever. Spiritual Mother, please pray for a new outpouring of the Holy Spirit of Love upon me. Bring anew the Holy Spirit of Courage to my days and nights on earth. Pray fervently that I may be made worthy of the promises of Christ.

---

*God alone is uncreated Eternal Energy. Authentic prayer opens us to the divine presence of God.

Chapter Three
KEYS TO CURES

I am the vine, you are the branches. Whoever remains in me and I in Him will bear much fruit, because without me you can do nothing.
—John 15:5

Cure for Exhaustion (Burn-out)

You cannot serve God and mammon. Therefore I tell you, do not worry about your life, what you will eat [or drink], or about your body, what you will wear. Is not life more than food and the body more than clothing? Look at the birds in the sky; they do not sow or reap, they gather nothing into barns, yet your heavenly Father feeds them. Are you not more important then they?
—Matthew 6:24–26

Q. SPIRITUAL MOTHER, I AM QUITE EXHAUSTED. CAN
YOU HELP ME?

A. My love for you is so vast that it is beyond your
present comprehension. You are my child. Allow
me to care for you as my child. Please hear my
voice. Please obey me. Choose the events in your
daily life with great care. It is not pleasing to God
to allow greed to keep you at work for the long
hours you are spending. Greed has many faces.
More prayer will give you the strength you seek.
Pray now for my children all over the world. Pray
and sacrifice for them.

Q. HOW SHALL I DO THAT?

A. Offer every moment of your life for their well-
being. Think of the lost children. Think of the
suffering children. Their lives are dear to me.
Their suffering brings great pain to my heart.

Q. IN WHAT WAY IS IT POSSIBLE FOR ME TO ACTUALLY
HELP THEM?

A. Your prayers and sacrifices activate the power
of God in their midst.

Q. WHAT KIND OF PRAYERS AND SACRIFICES DO YOU
WANT, DEAR SPIRITUAL MOTHER?

A. Choose your food with them in mind. Eat
what nourishes your body but not necessarily
what pleases you. Do not worry about your ap-

pearance so much. Exercise more. Exercise for them. They have no energy to exercise. Praise God the Father for them. Thank the Father for all the things you enjoy on their behalf.

Q. DO YOU WANT ME TO ENJOY MY LIFE FOR THEM?
A. Yes. A balanced life will give you health. If humanity had not upset the balance of nature by disobedience to God's Will, their life would be pleasant too. Every good thing you have is a gift of God. God wants you to enjoy these gifts. You must now share your enjoyment with my suffering children. Enjoy for them too. As you enjoy, see God's Love in your life and the lives of others.

Q. HOW WILL MY ENJOYMENT BRING RELIEF TO THE POOR AND SICK, THE LONELY AND ABANDONED?
A. Prayers of gratitude offered by you suffice for others too. You must share everything: your joy, your sorrow, your enjoyment, your work, your relationships, your recreation, your exercise. Many of my children have the gifts of recreation and exercise but do not use them. Many have the energy for recreation and exercise. You must use these gifts on behalf of all your brothers and sisters throughout the world for whom these gifts are impossible because of the selfishness of humanity.

Q. BLESSED MOTHER, I AM SAD THAT MANY HAVE SO LITTLE.

A. Your Father sees everything. He makes all things well. Praise our Father. Love our Father's generosity to all His children. Enjoy His very generous gifts to you with love and peace on behalf of all those who have no such opportunities. Your prayers on their behalf will unlock the oppression that binds them to despair. Never use anything of the earth except as a prayer. Share. Make your heart a living chalice of love.

Bear my Son to the world. God's earth is a house of prayer. He who works in God's house of prayer bears God to the world. Work with your hands, your heart, your mind. Then you will see God. Then you will hear Him. Then you will really know God, for God is lowly. God is poor. God is sick. God is hungry. God dies of neglect. God is the victim of abuse. God is the child of division. God is the daughter of slavery and the son of oppression. God is the least of His children for we are one, O my child. We are one. Pray and sing and serve before His face, for you now see His ways.

Those who rest now will not rest later. Their deeds will follow them.

Meditation

God is about to unveil segments of His vast unclaimed universe. Mysteries older than the earth unfold before my eyes. My heart is longing for pure Truth. I am a relentless, unrequited quest for love. We humans are eternal beings. Will only Eternal Love fill the depths of my longings? My quest expresses itself in many ways, some healthy and life-giving. Some expressions are fraught with seeds of self-destruction. Do I use all things of the earth as a prayer? Do I accept everything I have from the loving hand of God? Do I offer God love and thanksgiving? Do I actively seek obedience to His Will? Do I offer God everything I have for His honor and glory? Do I use all things with immense moderation in this way? Do I pray and serve others with global vision, embracing all God's people in my heart and my means? Do I share and share and share? Is my heart a poured-out chalice of God's Love?

Daily Application

With God's help, and by His strength, I shall never again eat or drink to excess. If tempted, I remember that Jesus was hungry and thirsty and lonely during His public life. One of His tortures during His passion was thirst. I shall never again work so that I am too weary to love, or exercise so that I am totally exhausted. I shall be pleasing to God by using the gifts He has provided for me with love and gratitude for my brothers and sisters who have no such gifts. I shall live in union with all humanity. The suffering deserve God's gifts too: I shall share with them. I shall use my home, workplace, recreation, and vacations for the honor and glory of our Father. With God's divine help, exercise will give me health for the work I must do to bring God's Kingdom on earth. Food and drink and employment will give me sustenance for the work I must do to build God's Kingdom on earth. Relationships will give me human love and human sorrow: Relationships will lead me to the depths of God's Love.

Prayer

With Your help, dear Lord, I share all with You and Yours for all is Yours. Teach me renewed mortification of the senses, dear Lord. The senses are subtle. When they are satiated, they are dulled to Your presence. When I fast and pray, I find You everywhere. When I fast and pray, I come near Truth, for You alone are Truth. You are beyond the senses. Help me to fast from the means of my own destruction, dear God of Love and Truth. You alone free me, for You alone are Lord. Help me rule my appetites, Lord, that You may rule my heart forever. I praise You and I thank You. You are my only life and my only Love. Amen.

Help me, please, to remember this Truth and live in it.

CURE FOR SADNESS

We fly to your protection, O Holy Mother of God.
Despise not our petitions for these necessities.
Deliver us from all dangers in body,
mind, and soul.
—*Ancient Prayer to the Mother of God*

Q. DEAR SPIRITUAL MOTHER, I FEEL VERY SAD AT
TIMES. CAN YOU HELP ME?
A. Stay consciously near to me, dear child. Experience my love for you. Love me. Concentrate
more on your prayers. Think about the words you
are saying. Be at peace with me. Spend more time
with me alone. I have much grace to give you.
Pray the Our Father that Jesus taught. Focus on all
His words as my Son speaks to your heart. When
you draw near to God in your heart, His joy falls
upon you and fills you.

Meditation

God knows all things. God can do all things.
God loves me.

Daily Application

I have spent too many hours embracing ideas, things, circumstances, places, and goals that pass away. From now on, I shall spend more time alone with my Spiritual Mother, seeking God's Kingdom that is all around me.

Prayer

Our Father who art in Heaven, hallowed be Your Name.

Your Kingdom come, Your will be done on earth as it is in Heaven. Give us this day our daily bread.

Forgive us our trespasses as we forgive those who trespass against us.

Lead us not into temptation but deliver us from evil. For Yours is the Kingdom and the Power and the Glory now and forever. Amen.

CURE FOR DISAPPOINTMENTS

The Divine Redeemer wishes to penetrate the soul
of every sufferer through the heart of His most
Holy Mother, the first and the most exalted
of all the redeemed.
—Pope John Paul II

Q. BLESSED MOTHER, PEOPLE AND SITUATIONS AND
EVENTS SOMETIMES DISAPPOINT ME. WHAT SHOULD I
DO?

A. Draw nearer to me, precious child of my heart.
The grapes of wrath come from poison in
mankind's heart. God's Heart is pure. God's Heart
is simple. God's Heart is Love. Only Love. Those
who know God's Love are gentle, for they know
God's gentleness. They share in His gentleness.
They understand His ways. Allow me to protect
you and to teach you of God's ways. Give your
heart to me and to no other creature. Give all your
relationships to me. Love all people as my dear
children. Accept with love the events and circumstances God places upon your path each day. Trust
me, your Spiritual Mother, to protect all your relationships and encounters. My graciousness rests
in my Son Jesus' Love for me and for you. Concentrate on your prayers. Listen for God's voice as
you pray. In that way you obtain guidance and
strength for your life on earth. Remain consciously in my presence. Dine on the joy of God's
Love. Worship at the font of His mercy. Mercy is
His Name, dear child of my heart.

Meditation

My Spiritual Mother speaks words of joy and
peace to my heart. Her song of love even now
echoes in my memory of golden times long ago.

Her dreams of goodness and peace among the peoples of the earth dance in my longings for what ought to be. With her, I call to the heights and depths of God's mercy: peace and joy and love to everyone of good will.

Daily Application

To succeed in obtaining solutions for the good life, I must arrange more private time to be alone and pray for eyes to see God and ears to hear His voice. From now on, nothing shall preempt my private time of prayer and silence.

Prayer

Spiritual Mother, please give me grace from the Heart of Jesus to be of good will, God's holy Will. May God's Kingdom come now in my life, in all my days and nights, in all my relationships and accomplishments and nothings too.

CURE FOR ANXIETY

Can any of you by worrying add a single moment to your life span? . . . Learn from the way the wild flowers grow. They do not work

or spin. But I tell you that not even Solomon in
all his splendor was clothed like one of them . . .
Do not worry about tomorrow; today will
take care of itself. . . .
—*Matthew 6:27–29, 34*

Q. BLESSED MOTHER, WHAT OF TOMORROW?
A. Do not fear. Live in my presence. Accept my love. Do not think of tomorrow. Tomorrow is only a field of illusion. Today is your gift. Enjoy my love and protection today. Each today well lived makes every tomorrow a vision of happiness in God's Heart of Love and providence.

Q. BLESSED MOTHER, WHAT OF YESTERDAY?
A. Leave every yesterday in the depths of God's mercy. Each today is a stepping stone to Paradise.

Meditation

Light shines in my heart when my Spiritual Mother speaks to me of God's unfathomable Love for me and for all His creatures. I am happy resting in divine Love that Mary brings to me. I delight in her Divine Son's holy Word, His holy Will, His holy Plan for my life.

Daily Application

Beginning now, I do not allow the tyranny of yesterday or the lure of tomorrow to interrupt God's presence with me. When anxiety creeps upon me like a thief in the night to steal my peace and joy, I shall flee in my mind and heart and will to the arms of Mary, my Spiritual Mother. Trusting her presence with me, I allow her to calm my fears with the power of her Son, the prince of peace and Lord of Lords.

Prayer

Stay with me, dear Mother of God. Keep me in your heart of love, for you alone are true daughter of God the Father, eternal Mother of God the Son, and cherished spouse of God the Holy Spirit. Spiritual Mother Most Powerful, keep me centered in God's Plan for my life forever. Amen.

CURE FOR DIFFICULTIES

By her maternal charity, [Mary] cares for the brethren of her Son, who still journey on earth surrounded by dangers and difficulties, until they are led [by God's Grace] into their blessed home.
—Second Vatican Council

Q. SPIRITUAL MOTHER, I AM EXPERIENCING DIFFI-
CULTY. WHAT SHALL I DO?

A. Do not fear. I am leading you away from
earthly joys into the Heart of my Son. Ask for
nothing but knowledge of God's perfect Will and
strength to accomplish the fulfillment of His Plan
for your life in all your days and nights on earth.
Disappointments lead you away from the valley of
earthly treasures that fade into dust. Trust my
heart, for it is your own Spiritual Mother's heart of
pure love. Trust my joy in you. Trust God's Plan in
your life. Trust my hopes for your family. Do not
fear. Live in my presence. Accept my love.

Meditation

Do I truly believe that God exists? Do I truly
believe that God loves me just as I am? Do I truly
trust God's Love and Providence? Do I accept the
Mother of Jesus Christ as my Spiritual Mother?
Will I allow her to be my Mother Most Wise?

Daily Application

What goals and aspirations do I cling to that
disturb God's presence in my life today? What
habits sabotage my good efforts today to grow in
God's Love? I will put more effort into discover-
ing Truth.

Prayer

Spiritual Mother, you are filled with God's Love and His choicest graces. Lead me as you desire, for I long to enter into the secret chambers of God and marvel at the vastness of His eternal wonders. Bring me to God's ways dressed in the joys of His Love and mercy, for you are my Blessed Mother Most Gentle and Wise. Thank you for your compassion and your tender love for me.

CURE FOR DISTRACTIONS

Let the soul of Holy Mary be in each of us to
glorify the Lord. Let the spirit of Holy Mary
be in each of us to rejoice in God.
—*St. Ambrose*

Q. SPIRITUAL MOTHER, I AM TOO EASILY DISTRACTED IN MY LIFE. CAN YOU HELP ME?

A. Distractions die with the body and do not resurrect with it. They are trials and tests of faithfulness. Stay focused on God's Will for you. Do not appear "holy" to others. Follow only the path of Jesus. Ponder Jesus' admonitions to the Scribes and Pharisees (MATTHEW 23:1–28). Be cheerful always. Do not draw attention to yourself. Be humble, dear child, as I am humble. Serve others as a sign of your love for God. Endure distractions patiently. Do not embrace them. Entrust your spirit to God's love and mercy. Rest in my love. In that way you shall always know peace.

Meditation

Do I value my indwelling spirit properly? Do I assign eternal value to my time, my goals, my relationships, my behavior, my hopes and dreams?

Daily Application

From now on, I guard my spiritual life carefully from prying eyes that look but do not love. I exert great effort to avoid the outward appearance of "holiness." I refuse, in any way, to draw attention to myself. To appear "holy" to others is to slight God, who alone is holy. To appear "holy" is to make of myself a major distraction. I will not allow myself, or others, to become a golden calf (DEUTERONOMY 9:15–17) of distraction.

Prayer

My Spiritual Mother Mary, I turn to you and ask your assistance in all the moments of each day and night on this earth, and ever after. Intercede for me always with your Divine Son Jesus. Kindly ask Him to grant me conscious awareness of God's divine presence in my life, and in all that lives. Help my heart to become my chapel, where God dwells in splendor. Let the power of my love become my votive lamp. Surround me with the perfume of your presence at every moment, for surely He who is mighty has done great things for you and holy is His Name. May I please love all people, places, and things only for God, in God, and with God forever.

*C*URE FOR *I*NCONVENIENCES

I have told you this so that you might have peace
in me. In the world you will have trouble, but
take courage, I have conquered the world.
—John 16:33

Q. BLESSED MOTHER, I AM ENCOUNTERING INCONVE-
NIENCES THAT MAKE MY LIFE UNCOMFORTABLE: ILLNESS,
WARS, NATURAL DISASTERS, CORRUPT OFFICIALS, VIO-
LENCE, COMPLEX REGULATIONS, TRAFFIC, POLLUTION,
INCLEMENT WEATHER, ECONOMIC UNCERTAINTY, AND
PERSONAL PROBLEMS OF EVERY KIND. HOW CAN I FIND
PEACE WITH ALL THESE INCONVENIENCES OVER WHICH I
HAVE LITTLE OR NO CONTROL?

A. Change your focus. Love my Son Jesus more. Be faithful to Him as He is always faithful to you. Be constant in your love as Jesus is constant in His love for you. Obey our Father's Will. He is your Father too, just as He is Jesus' Father. Sing a new song in your heart of trust in God's presence in your life. Open your eyes to the beauties that surround you at each moment. Listen to the sweetness of the birds that praise our Father. Feel the gentleness of the winds that caress your face. Accept the divine Truth that you are loved unconditionally forever. Trust God's immense, unfathomable, eternal Love for you. Remain peaceful as God's Plan for your life unfolds around you.

Meditation

If I am true believer, I accept my path in this life. I shall be, obey, sing, listen, feel, accept, trust, remain. Each inconvenience is an opportunity to trust God's divine Love and Providence in my life.

Daily Application

Today, I shall observe all inconveniences of any kind as an opportunity to find God's loving Plan in my midst.

Prayer

Spiritual Mother, today I seek the kindness of your hand in mine. Today I desire the quiet firmness of your faith, of your trust in resurrection that makes new creation. Comfort me in my doubts. Console me with awareness of the presence of your Divine Child, who is the Word made flesh, the light of the world, the object of my desires, and Lord of my life. Spiritual Mother, bless His holy Name for me forever. Jesus, please shine the light of Your Love into every inconvenience I ever encounter. Jesus, Son of God and son of Mary, You are the source of peace. Jesus, You are my peace.

CURE FOR PANIC

> *[Jesus] went up on the mountain by himself to*
> *pray. When it was evening he was there alone.*
> —*Matthew 14:23*

Q. SPIRITUAL MOTHER, MY PATH CONTINUES TO BE STREWN WITH DREADFUL MOMENTS WHEN I EXPERIENCE PANIC. WHAT SHOULD I DO?
A. Look into my eyes of unconditional love, dear child, and know that my son, Jesus Christ, is God. Jesús Christ is our Savior. Look now into the eyes

of our Savior, my child. Accept His power in your depths. Allow His unconditional Love to pour into your heart now. See Jesus, the King of all Kings. Allow your divine Brother, Jesus, to lift you into His Sacred Heart, where all the beauty of creation sings and dances as you play before the face of God. You are my precious child. You are beautiful. You belong to God alone. Come to me now, dear child of beauty, and Love. Allow me to rock you in the sweet caresses of God's joy in you, to sing to you of God's hopes for you. All that is not well will be well. God our Father gave you to Jesus before He made the world (JOHN 17:5, 24). Not one of the little ones entrusted to Jesus will be lost (JOHN 17:12). I place you in the arms of your Divine Brother now. Jesus loves you. His Love is power. Use it wisely.

Meditation

My Spiritual Mother desires to take me to the heights of the mountain of prayer to encounter Jesus. On the summit of the mountain of prayer, I too shall find our Father's Will and enter the Heart of Jesus. No path is too difficult for me if I remain in the Heart of Jesus.

Daily Application

Today, in every circumstance, I trust God's presence and His merciful Heart. I trust God's power of Love, for I am but a little child of our Father. Jesus bears the solutions to all the problems I carry. Today, I give Jesus my burdens so that I may rest serene upon His Heart.

Prayer

Lord Jesus, Your Blessed Mother has given me to You. She reminds me that God our Father gave me to You before the world began. Lord Jesus, please carry me to the mountain of God's holy Will. In God's Will alone is my beauty, my power, my peace. Lord Jesus, open my intellect to receive Your instructions. Lord Jesus, strengthen my will to obey Your commands. Lord Jesus, enlighten my being with Your wisdom that I may truly experience Your joy, Your peace, and Your Love. Lord Jesus, gentle and meek, may I hold Your Sacred Hand and sing in the depths of Truth, may I rest serene upon Your Sacred Heart and gently offer all praise and glory to our Father, for You are His beloved Son, begotten through the power of the Holy Spirit. Lord Jesus, thank you for Your Mother, my Mother Most Loving.

CURE FOR INDECISIVENESS

*Jesus answered, "Amen, amen, I say to you, no
one can enter the kingdom of God without
being born of water and spirit. What is born of flesh
is flesh, and what is born of spirit is spirit.
Do not be amazed that I told you, 'You must
be born from above.' The wind blows where it
wills, and you can hear the sound it makes, but
you do not know where it comes from or
where it goes; so it is with everyone who
is born of the Spirit.*
—John 3:5–8

Q. BLESSED MOTHER, I AM AT ANOTHER TURNING
POINT IN MY LIFE. DECISIONS NEED TO BE MADE. WILL
YOU HELP ME CHOOSE THE RIGHT PATH?

A. Pray to the Holy Spirit for guidance. Pray
more. Love more. A throne shall be prepared in
mercy, and you may sit upon it in Truth. Jesus
alone is the Way and the Truth and the Light for
your journey on the earth. Jesus is Life. Be like Jesus. Obey only the Will of our Father. Live in the
Holy Spirit of Love. Pray, dear child. Pray with me
now. Pray always. Draw ever nearer to Jesus and
you shall find Truth.

Meditation

Prayer changes things in Heaven and on earth too. Prayer is my daily decision. Prayer is my key to the good life. The Holy Spirit dwelling within me knows how to pray in me. My decision to walk alone outside the Will of God for me is sacredly respected by God. Pain brings awareness that I do not walk with God. Then I dwell in solitary confinement, self-condemned to relentless, self-inflicted spiritual torture that ever so cruelly maims and mocks and defaces my struggling young spirit that pines for freedom. God's Will for me is Truth. Truth alone is freedom. Jesus is Truth.

Daily Application

There is a right way and a wrong way to do everything. There is an easy way and a hard way to live. I must allow Jesus to break into my time and space and rescue me from unconscious torture chambers of illusion. The Scriptures show me the way. I must find and obey God's Will by praying my way through Christ's Word, His life, His promises. Today, and every day from now on, I prayerfully read the Bible. Christ's Word is my path to the good life.

Prayer

Come, Lord Jesus, come and rescue me. Come, Holy Spirit. Cover my thoughts and words and deeds with the power of Your Divine Love and mercy. O Most Holy Spirit, flowing forth from God the Father and God the Son, guard me and guide me in all my ways. Jesus, You are my Savior. Save me, Jesus. Please reveal Yourself and your ways to me, Lord Jesus. Your ways alone are living Truth.

Chapter Four

KEYS TO HEALING

*I, [God] gentle first Truth, name the situation, the time,
and the place, consolations or trials, whatever is necessary
for salvation and to bring souls to the perfection for which
I choose them. . . . [E]verything I give is for love, and
they therefore should accept everything with reverence.*
—St. Catherine of Siena

Cure for Ingratitude

*Then the soldiers of the governor took Jesus inside
the praetorium and gathered the whole cohort
around him. They stripped off his clothes and
threw a scarlet military cloak about him. Weaving
a crown out of thorns, they placed it on his head,
and a reed in his right hand. And kneeling before
him, they mocked him saying, "Hail, King of the
Jews!" They spat upon him and took the reed
and kept striking him on the head. And when*

they had mocked him, they stripped him of
the cloak, dressed him in his own clothes,
and led him off to crucify him.
—*Matthew 27:27–31*

Q. SPIRITUAL MOTHER, I DO GRACIOUS AND SACRIFI-
CIAL THINGS FOR MY FAMILY AND FOR OTHERS THAT NO
ONE EVER SEEMS TO NOTICE OR TO APPRECIATE. I
SOMETIMES FEEL MY HEART BEGIN TO HARDEN AT SUCH
INGRATITUDE. YET, PARADOXICALLY, I HAVE JUST BEGUN
TO NOTICE CERTAIN PEOPLE WHO ARE ESPECIALLY KIND
TO ME IN PAINFUL MOMENTS.

A. Appreciate them. They serve me when they
serve you. They make my Son happy. They are
dear to me. They are our gift to you. Know that
every little or great thing you do to serve others is
dear to my Son. All that is unseen will be seen.
Give your heart to Jesus. Give your sacrifices to
Him, for in Jesus alone is life. Trust the promises of
Jesus. Know that whatever you do to the least of
your brethren, you do before the face of God. Do
you see now, my child, why you may never judge
a person? God alone knows the hearts of His
children.

Meditation

All the good things I have in my life come
from God. All difficult things I encounter are per-

mitted by God for my growth and development, or for someone else. My Spiritual Mother is here with me at all times. Her Divine Son Jesus is my Lord and Savior. He never leaves me. He sees and hears and knows everything I think and say and do. Jesus is my Divine Brother. I desperately need Jesus. Everyone needs Jesus.

Daily Application

Jesus is the Divine Architect who makes all things new, even me. Today, I hand to Jesus everything in my life that needs to be repaired. I give Jesus each act of kindness, each little pain and sorrow that I feel when others forget my efforts and sacrifices for them. From today on, I shall trust Jesus to make all the people, things, and relationships in my life bright beacons of peace and happiness.

Prayer

Spiritual Mother Most Gracious, pray that I may always hear the voice of God, trust and thank Him for His goodness, unite myself with His Will in great gratitude and joy and peace, bless the people, events, and circumstances that unfold around me, knowing all flows from His Divine Love. May I trust and live, in difficult moments, as

Jesus lived and taught. May I love the face of God with gentle, heartfelt, loving concern and care for all the people, places, and things, dressed in costumes made of earth, that hide the living face of God within.

Cure for Stress

And it happened that while they were conversing
and debating, Jesus himself drew near and
walked with them, but their eyes were prevented
from recognizing him.
—*Luke 24:15–16*

Q. SPIRITUAL MOTHER, I AM EXPERIENCING STRESS IN MY LIFE: IN MY FAMILY AND MY WORK.

A. Do not be afraid. You have taken your eyes away from the Kingdom of God. God alone brings solutions to all your problems. Do not focus on your problems. Focus only on God's Will for you now, moment by moment. In these days of stress, increase your prayer time. Accept all your responsibilities with respect for God's holy Will. Do only your part: Faithfully fulfill all your obligations. When you encounter difficulties, turn to God for light and guidance. Trust God. His power is adequate to solve all difficulties. Pray as a family as best you can. Families have wars because they do not pray together. Peace vanishes in any place where God's presence is not honored. Those who pray know God. Those who know God love God. Those who love God live and work in peace. They never want. Love my Son Jesus more. Be calm. Be patient. Be courageous. Await me. Listen carefully for my voice. I pray for you always. Do your part.

Meditation

It is more dangerous today than ever before to wander from God's presence. To walk with God, I must subject myself to His Divine authority. His commandments, His Divine principles, His statutes are written upon every human heart. Even nature is their subject. He alone, who is mighty, allows me to bask in His Divine Attributes.

Daily Application

I pray to cherish God's holy ordinances. They are gentle, protective walls that guard me from blindly stepping off a hidden, haunted precipice, designed by the evil one below, who writhes in decay, as this long-awaited Light of Christ unmasks his lies and deceit. God's rules protect me. I choose His protection by seeking God's loving commandments of Love. I accept God's protection by obeying His great commandments of Love. To rest within the safety of God's protective walls is to eliminate stress.

Prayer

Blessed Mother of Jesus, my Spiritual Mother, help me to trust God's Love, kindness, presence with me, around me, and in me. Help me to believe, in the difficult moments, that God will indeed bring beauty, goodness, and abiding Love out of even the most horrible conflicts. Help me to comprehend that nothing is impossible with God, who alone is holy, almighty, perfect Love. Spiritual Mother Most Wise, sing psalms, hymns, and spiritual songs for me and with me. Mother Most Loving, place profound gratitude in my heart for God's perfect faithfulness. Thank you for being here with me, for showing me that through the power of God's Love, all that is not well will indeed be well, for teaching me that when I walk with God, He gives me enjoyment, abiding peace, and eternal love. God's word is Truth.

CURE FOR CONFLICTS

Let the word of Christ dwell in you richly, as in
all wisdom you teach and admonish one another,

*singing psalms, hymns, and spiritual songs with
gratitude in your hearts to God.*
—*Colossians 3:16*

Q. BLESSED MOTHER, WHY AM I ENCOUNTERING SO
MANY CONFLICTS EVERYWHERE?

A. I will not abandon you in your conflicts. Will
you abandon me? Do not always look for things
that are pleasant. You shall find me in many places
that are not pleasant. I am the faithful Mother. I
bring solutions to all human problems: I bring Jesus.
Under the haunted, hidden precipice, predators
hold shackles ready for their prey. Do not weep
and gnash your teeth: summon Jesus. The Good
Shepherd leads a rescue mission into the depths of
darkness: Jesus sets the captive free. Obey His word!
Follow Jesus out of bondage. Return with honor
to the land of the living. Surrender quickly to the
creative hand of God that makes all things new in
endless beauty before adoring eyes throughout creation.
To love is to know Jesus well. Jesus, the Divine
Physician, refashions and restores. Rejoice,
little children of God! Rejoice, O angels and saints
of the Kingdom of God! We are one family in
Love! Laugh and sing and play. My Son Jesus is the
sinner's delight. Jesus is the Good News. We are
one.

Meditation

God covenants faithfulness and kindness to those who obey His Will. It is a spiritual challenge to recognize God's Love and kindness amid the pain of sickness, violence, poverty, misunderstandings, injustice. My Spiritual Mother reminds me constantly: God loves His children unconditionally. The Apostle Peter learned from Jesus: Every day we fall short of perfect compliance with God's holy ordinances seventy times seven. Like Peter, we desperately need Jesus.

Daily Application

Today, I realize that Jesus saves us. But I must choose Jesus and follow His path. I actively choose Jesus' ways in all my thoughts, words, and actions.

Prayer

Hail Mary, my Spiritual Mother, how gentle is your voice! Hail Mary, my Mother Most Loving, how kindly is your wisdom! Pray with me now for each member of my family, those I admire and those I find difficult. Bring the power of your Divine Son's Love to my home and workplace. Teach us the miracle of gracious tolerance. Help us to create an agenda in harmony with God's holy Will. Ask Him to change our hearts now, to touch us and awaken us to His loving presence in us and around us and with us. Help me to trust God's Plan, God's unconditional Love for me and all His creation, to see the deeper value of each person in my family and in my workplace, to accept God's holy and perfect Plan for our happiness now and for all eternity.

*C*URE FOR *F*AILURE

[The angel] said to them, "Do not be amazed!
You seek Jesus of Nazareth, the crucified.
He has been raised."
—Mark 16:6

Q. BLESSED MOTHER, WHY DO I EXPERIENCE FAILURE, EVEN WITH THE BEST OF PREPARATIONS AND INTENTIONS?
A. Things of the earth will never please you. They will never satisfy you. Avoid things that take your mind off God and keep your eyes on the earth. Go back to simplicity. Live in the center of God's Will. God alone brings victory out of every defeat.

Meditation

The earth is our global village. My behavior impacts my well-being, the well-being of everyone else and the planet too. What impacts the earth impacts all living things. Wisdom requires me to live in gracious toleration: respect for all life and not just mine. Knowledge teaches me the uniqueness of each human being, the planet we all inhabit and the entire cosmos. As my own personal family struggles to grow in love and harmony, our global family is struggling to find common ground. We seek solutions to every human, ecological, and universal need. Everyone is poor, for the earth is poor. Everyone is sick, for the earth is sick. Everyone is lonely, for the earth is lonely. We are one. Love is the only common language that binds all living things. Non-love is the only failure.

Daily Application

Heaven is our goal. Nothing else has lasting value. God has commanded us to subdue the earth. Today, when I feel that the earth has subdued me, I look to Jesus on the cross for solutions to my failure. Jesus' crucifixion looked like a failed life to all His apostles but John. Today, I give all my failures to Jesus on the cross. In His Heart, my mistakes are promises of resurrection of all I hold dear. Today, through my failures, I am learning that each human being must voluntarily, or involuntarily, spend time alone before God. God created each of us for Himself. He demands that we love everyone and everything (including ourselves and our failures) in His Name, for Him (1 JOHN 4:21). In God, there is only victory, even for me.

Prayer

Dear Spiritual Mother, I do desire to live in simplicity. Show me the things I really need, and those more burden than pleasure. Gently guide me daily to wisely choose God's gifts that fill my heart with joyful song. Direct me quickly away from places and people and things that disturb gracious graces God intends for me. Kindly keep me always in the center of God's Plan for me, never anywhere else. Please arrange my life that I may truly love only God's Will forever.

CURE FOR MISJUDGMENTS

What profit is there for one to gain the whole world yet lose or forfeit himself?
—Luke 9:25

Q. BLESSED MOTHER, I AM SO BUSY THAT I HAVE NO TIME TO PROPERLY EVALUATE CERTAIN DECISIONS. CAN YOU HELP ME SO THAT I DO NOT MAKE COSTLY MISJUDGMENTS?

A. Be careful with your time. Do not waste it. You do not have that much left. Love God. Trust God. Heaven is closer than you think. I am Queen of Peace. I am your eternal Mother. Accept my peace, for I am the Mother of God. You shall find peace only in God's perfect Will. My work is God's work. When you do God's work, you have adequate time for His perfect Will. You have time for nothing else. God's justice cleanses your life of all that is not of Him, for Him, and with Him. Praise God's justice. God's justice is Love.

Meditation

The only reality that lives forever is love. Love for God's people, God's earth, God's animals, God's trees, God's rivers, God's wind, God's sky, God's vast universe, God's joys, God's sorrows, God's rewards, and God's vengeance.*

---

*Vengeance is God's alone. God's vengeance is not like human vengeance. God has no cruelty. God's vengeance cleanses. God's vengeance purifies. No cruelty flows from God's hand, for God is Love.

Daily Application

I remind myself that the longest human life measures little more than one hundred good years, yet our choices during our human life impact how our indwelling spirit lives forever. Today, I reevaluate my priorities in light of my eternal goals. How much time do I spend each day doing things that are unnecessary and help no one? This time I shall reclaim for prayer, recreation, and service to others. How peace-filled is my work? Today, I seek to work only as God would have me work. I give my work to God as my prayer. How blessed are my relationships? Are they God-centered? I give my relationships to God as my prayer. I seek light and strength to use my life only as God desires.

Prayer

Spiritual Mother, my Queen of Peace, you are Queen of my heart. Help me always to surrender anew to the presence of God in all that lives. Teach me the mysteries of God's peace in the world. Turn my eyes and will and time to the glories of God. Show me ways to bring joy to God, to God's creatures in Heaven and on the earth, to the angels and saints who surround you and me constantly. Allow me to appreciate the earth that houses me now and all the beauties that God shares with those who have eyes to see Him and ears to hear

Him in the world. Mother of divine grace, please awaken me totally to Truth. Help me to give God my life as a blank check for His use as He wills.

Cure for Mistakes

If anyone wishes to come after me, he must deny
himself and take up his cross daily and
follow me. For whoever wishes to save his
life will lose it, but whoever loses his life
for my sake will save it.
—*Luke 9:23–24*

Q. BLESSED MOTHER, I HAVE MANY THINGS TO DO. I HAVE MADE POOR CHOICES. HOW CAN I DEAL WITH PAINFUL MISTAKES?
A. Things of the earth do not go to Heaven, but they can keep you from Heaven. Be careful. Be on guard always. Turn away from too many things. Become selective. Pray more. Love more. Listen for my voice before you act. Obey me carefully. I love you. Please prayerfully read the Scriptures. In that way, you sanctify your time. Jesus is the Way and the Truth and the Light for your journey on the earth. Please follow Jesus.

Meditation

I need the great gift of wisdom at all times. Scripture teaches me to plead for the gift of wisdom.

Daily Application

Today, I guard carefully the way I spend my time. I consciously eliminate activities that bear me no fruit for the Kingdom of Heaven.

Prayer

Spiritual Mother, you are the Seat of Wisdom. I desperately need wisdom. Help me to love God as He deserves and desires of me. You obeyed God's holy and mysterious Will: In so doing, you have brought the glories of God's presence to the nations in your Divine Son Jesus. You continuously experience the gift of Heaven. Cherished Spouse of the Holy Spirit, please send the Holy Spirit of Truth to my dreams, goals, mornings, and evenings of longing. Whisper wisdom as you sing sweet lullabies of God's Holy Spirit over all the earth, my eternal Spiritual Mother. Please give me wisdom, dearest Mother of God, for your Divine Son is forever the source of wisdom. Please give me Jesus.

CURE FOR LONELINESS

Do not let your hearts be troubled. Have faith in
God; have faith also in me. In my Father's house
there are many dwelling places. If there were not,
would I have told you that I am going to prepare
a place for you? And if I go and prepare a place
for you, I will come back again and take you to
myself, so that where I am you also may be.
—John 14:1–3

Q. BLESSED MOTHER, I LOOK FOR GOD EVERYWHERE,
IN PEOPLE, PLACES, AND EVENTS, YET I AM VERY LONELY.
WHY?
A. You cannot find God with your mind, for it
is a labyrinth with many avenues of deception.
Love God. Obey God. Be faithful to God. You
know God. Come to know Him better through
His word. Jesus is the Way and the Truth and the
Light. Jesus is life. Turn to Jesus with your heart,
your mind, and your will. Trust the promises of
Jesus.

Meditation

My soul yearns for the living God. My heart
and my mind and my flesh war against the longing

of my spirit for the courts of the Lord of all the living.

Daily Application

Today, I actively search for God everywhere. He promised those who seek Him find Him. Today, I will to obey Jesus in thought, word, and deed. His word is life-giving.

Prayer

Dear Mother of the Word, how sweet are the dwelling places of the Lord. Yet how long are the nights of doubt that darken my path. Give me peace, dear Mother of the living God. Give me wisdom to see always the divine presence of God in all that lives. Give me Jesus forever.

Cure for Materialism

The beginning of wisdom is the fear of the Lord.
—Proverbs 9:10

Q. BLESSED MOTHER, WHAT ABOUT ALL THE POOR?
A. They are poor because you do not share. Be gracious to God's poor.

Q. WHAT WOULD YOU LIKE ME TO DO FOR THE POOR, BLESSED MOTHER?

A. Pray for the grace to give away what you do not need with a generous heart filled with love. Then you will be free.

Q. WHAT ABOUT THINGS I MAY NOT NEED TODAY BUT POSSIBLY WILL NEED TOMORROW? SHOULDN'T I SAVE SUCH THINGS?

A. Embrace prudence. Remember that God requires you to be a faithful steward of *all* He has entrusted to you. There is no tomorrow. There is only today. When you live in simplicity, you will be happy and God will fill you full. Be sensitive first to the needs of your family and community. In your newfound freedom you will be an instrument of God's Love, His joy, and His generosity.

Q. BLESSED MOTHER, ARE YOU CERTAIN THAT GOD WANTS ME TO GIVE AWAY WHAT I DO NOT USE TODAY? I DO ENJOY MANY THINGS THAT I DO NOT NEED.

A. Pray for wisdom to be a good and faithful steward of *His* assets, for they are not yours. Be faithful to God's ways, my child. Obey God peacefully and be filled with trust. Pray for strength to accept God's ways. Trust God's Love totally in every decision you make. Then you will know how to share with wisdom and love. You will know what to keep for yourself and what to relinquish for the use of others.

Q. BLESSED MOTHER, WHAT IF IT FEELS PAINFUL TO OBEY GOD'S WILL?

A. Always ponder how my beloved Jesus obeyed His Father. Use my strength to be a good and humble servant. Remember constantly that Jesus is the Way and the Truth and the Life. He is light for your journey on earth.

Meditation

I must remember always that Jesus is the Way and the Truth and the Life. In His light, I see almsgiving and sharing as vital parts of every spiritual journey. To actively embrace almsgiving and sharing is the highest wisdom. Otherwise, our good God will impose this spiritual discipline upon me from His mighty hand of Love. Simplicity is my goal. Almsgiving and sharing are the gentle path to the Kingdom of God. Only what I give away in love is mine to keep in the eternal realms of divine peace, joy, and Love.

Daily Application

My life path has many people upon it. Today, I shall be careful, very careful of the example I set. Many follow me. More than I can know. Nothing must be wasted. Everything has a use in God's Kingdom. I shall begin now to give away everything I do not need. I shall allow others to use what I do not need. To waste offends God. To hoard destroys me, and those I love.

Prayer

Blessed Mother, help me to be poor in spirit. Help me to live as Jesus lived. Show me how to eliminate everything that is not of Jesus or for Jesus or with Jesus. The time is now. Help me to live in absolute peace as you did when you walked the earth as I do now. Make me a conduit of God's great Plan for His people of the earth. Allow me to choose only God's Will, nothing more, but never anything less.

Cure for Overwork

All their works are performed to be seen. . . .
They love places of honor. . . .
—*Matthew 23:5,6*

Q. BLESSED MOTHER, I AM VERY BUSY. MY WORK IS NEVER DONE. I HAVE GOALS, BUT JUST AS ONE IS AC-COMPLISHED, ANOTHER RISES. WHAT SHOULD I DO?
A. When you perform God's work, you have time for everything. Jesus adorns with things that are everlasting. You adorn with transitory things of

the earth. Avoid places of temptation. I was simple and unknown when I was on the earth. Learn from me, for my Son is God. Help one another not to need so much. Earthly accomplishments are deceptive. Earthly treasures are soon dust in forgotten places. Love alone lives forever. Never grieve the Heart of Love for any reason. Love alone is life.

Meditation

I hear God's gentle voice of Heaven's Love. God calls to me, but I hurry to the marketplace, to the workplace, to the highways and byways of the world's allures only to find my heart crying out to highest Heaven in every moment of awakening.

Daily Application

If today I hear His voice, I shall respond, regardless of the cost, for God alone is my life, my only reality. Today, I gently begin the abandonment of all that is not of God, for God, with God. I will no longer frequent frivolous places that absorb my time, assets, and peace.

Prayer

Spiritual Mother, Queen of Peace, please bring your Son Jesus, the source of peace, to fill my heart with newborn Love so tender and so sweet for precious things of God that last. Give me Love, sweet Mother of the Lord. Please give me peace. Give me Jesus, my prince of peace.

Part Two

FINDING PARADISE

AND I HEARD A GREAT VOICE FROM THE
THRONE, SAYING: BEHOLD THE TABERNA-
CLE OF GOD WITH MEN, AND HE WILL
DWELL WITH THEM. AND THEY SHALL BE
HIS PEOPLE; AND GOD HIMSELF WITH
THEM SHALL BE THEIR GOD. AND GOD
SHALL WIPE AWAY ALL TEARS FROM THEIR
EYES: AND DEATH SHALL BE NO MORE,
NOR MOURNING, NOR CRYING, NOR
SORROW SHALL BE ANYMORE, FOR THE
FORMER THINGS ARE PASSED AWAY.

•

—*Revelation 21:3–4*

PEACE PRAYER FOR THE MILLENNIUM

The Source of Peace is near.
He whispers in the wind and makes our earth
His Holy House.
We belong to Him who is our only Love.

See, His angels draw near now
to pluck the thorns
that pierce our hands with greed.
Stingers in our eyes they see.
"Be gone distortion," they all beam
and lust and avarice and sloth give up and leave.

When I see the Source of Peace,
Joy shall be my name.
Peace shall be my claim.

Dance my trembling heart.
Sing and play and pray today.
The Source of Peace comes here to stay.

I shall find Him now.
I know His Way.
He hides in gifts of love we bring
to Him this day.

Chapter Five

SPARKLING JEWELS

*Though we are always in the presence of God, it seems to
me the manner is different with those who practice prayer,
for they are aware that He is looking at them.*
—St. Teresa of Avila

SUFFERING TURNED TO JOY

*Amen, amen, I say to you, you will weep and
mourn, while the world rejoices; you will grieve,
but your grief will become joy. When a woman is
in labor, she is in anguish because her hour has
arrived; but when she has given birth to a child,
she no longer remembers the pain because of her
joy that a child has been born into the world.
So you also are now in anguish. But I will
see you again, and your hearts will rejoice, and
no one will take your joy away from you.*
—John 16:20–22

Q. SPIRITUAL MOTHER, WHY MUST I SUFFER?

A. God loves you. Nothing He allows you to suffer will be too much for you. Praise Him. God calls you to Heaven. Your path is faithfulness. Trust God. Look to nothing else. It is through trust in God's providence that you are able to experience suffering in peace. Heaven is for those who trust God. Rest in my heart of love. Allow me to remain in your conscious awareness and speak to you of the wonders of God's Love.

Meditation

I know the bitter bark of winter yields brilliant blossoms of spring and wealth and warmth in summer, and fragrant, flowering foliage of fall. I choose to disturb my foolish fears with continuous, conscious commitments to trust in the joys of new life that mysteriously but certainly grow out of this present pain that perturbs my patience.

Daily Application

Today, I am being tested in the fire of God's Love. If my love were purer, I would taste the sweetness of God's ways in this suffering. Today, I will find joy to give, a song to serve, a smile to soothe. Tears are my sign that God makes all things new in countless mornings of hope. Tears water

His garden in my heart and drive away the darkness. I tearfully surrender to God's Plan for my life. His Will is my nourishment. His ways are my joy. My tears are my trust in resurrection.

Prayer

Spiritual Mother, illumine within me fathomless depths of faith to accept the truths of God's divine Love for me and all I hold dear. Where you are, my Queen of Angels, so also is God. Please ask God, who is King of kindness and Lord of Love, that I may truly believe and trust and love in His Kingdom of kindness and Love now and forever. In the meantime, my ever sorrow is my meager sign of faith and hope and love.

FOREBODING TURNED TO COURAGE

In the world you will have trouble, but take
courage, I have conquered the world.
—John 16:33

Q. SPIRITUAL MOTHER MOST PRUDENT, WHY AM I AFRAID THAT TERRIBLE THINGS MAY HAPPEN?
A. My child, your anguish offends God. All that comes to you is God's gift to you. God sees you as

you were, as you are, as you will be. Bless all that comes upon the path you must travel to God's Kingdom. Bless and love. Then you taste the sweetness of God's ways. God's ways are Heaven on earth. Love God. Never look away from Him. Never surrender to fear. God is always with you. Trust God. Rest in God's promises. God never fails.

Meditation

Sometimes it is difficult to believe God loves me. When I see possibilities for destruction of my dreams, goals, longings, and accomplishments, I feel quite afraid. It is not easy to see the fruit of my life's efforts crushed in the wine press of God's Will. The jaws of death foreclose only on illusions. I choose to build on God's rock, not mine. All that crosses my path in this life is God's sign of Love, only Love.

Daily Application

Only in God and through God and with God do I experience nurturing, satisfying, life-giving eternal Love. Today will I give up all my illusions?

Prayer

O God, I wince again and again as I call to you. Do I begin to understand Your ways? You alone are Holy. You alone are power. You alone are justice. You alone reward. You alone chastise. All that I see, all that I experience during my journey on Your earth, You have allowed. Illumine bright the ways of Your Love. Thank you, Spiritual Mother, for standing with me as I speak to Almighty God in this way. No human love ever satisfies an eternal human being. I see that now. Only eternal Love will do. All Love flows from the Heart of God and returns to Him (1 JOHN 4:8). My Lord and my God, You alone are eternal Love. Thank you for the courage to face this reality.

ESTRANGEMENT TURNED TO REUNION

. . . But I am not alone, because the Father is with me. I have told you this so that you might have peace in me.
—John 16:32–33

Q. BLESSED MOTHER, SOMETIMES I FEEL QUITE ALONE, EVEN WHEN I'M SURROUNDED WITH PEOPLE AND THINGS I THINK I LOVE. WHY IS THIS SO?
A. Dear child, be still. Be silent. See God in every circumstance of your life. You have no reason to be so sorrowful, or so lonely. Try more diligently to see God everywhere. You know God never

leaves you. You are not separate from God. Please acknowledge God's divine presence in all that lives. I am here for you now. Do you want me to lead you to Jesus? God loves you beyond your capacity to understand. Dare to be alone with God.

Q. BLESSED MOTHER, HOW DO I DARE TO BE ALONE WITH GOD?
A. Journey beyond your senses. God told you: "I AM." He calls to you. Allow me to bring you to Him in the silence of your heart.

Meditation

I acknowledge God truly present in all that lives. His word teaches us that God alone is Life.

Daily Application

Today, I allow my Spiritual Mother more control over my decisions and activities so that she may lead me to Jesus. I will give fifteen minutes each day to Mary that belong to no one else. I will guard those fifteen minutes as my lifeline to eternal life.

Prayer

Dear God, wherever there is life, please grace me to praise and glorify Your divine presence with profound gratitude. Dear God, may Your perfect

Will be done. May I enter Your Kingdom of Love now? Please give me eyes to see You in the world, ears to hear You in the world, and a heart that beats for You alone.

WEARINESS TURNED TO VIGOR

So do not worry and say, "What are we to eat?"
or "What are we to drink?" or "What are we to
wear?" All these things the pagans seek.
Your heavenly Father knows that you need
them all. But seek first the Kingdom [of God]
and His righteousness, and all these things
will be given to you besides.
—Matthew 6:31–33

Q. SPIRITUAL MOTHER, I CONTINUE TO BE WEARY, TOTALLY EXHAUSTED.

A. Surrender your spirit into the hands of God that the persecutions of the times may touch it not. Take care of your bodily needs. God gave you your body. Love it not in the ways of the flesh but in the ways of the Spirit. Pray and fast and abandon yourself to my motherly care. Focus your eyes on the presence of God in all that lives. Accept God's Love and providence that you may walk clothed in His divine strength. Give your burdens to Jesus your Brother.

Meditation

The life of Jesus teaches me that to accept God's Love, I must accept His resignation at the human failings all around me. The Holy Spirit enlightens me that God knit my body for me in my mother's womb. My body is my good and faithful servant while I am on the earth. Am I a good steward of my body?

Daily Application

Today I inquire of myself: Am I am so self-righteous that I see faults in everyone but me? Today, I pray for eyes to see God's glories in every person, place, and thing, including myself. Today, I will carefully nourish and nurture the body that God has given to me. I will cherish my body as my good and faithful servant. I will be a loving and generous master. I will do unto others as I do unto myself.

Prayer

Mary, my Mother, please pray with me to Jesus now. Lord Jesus Christ, Son of the Living God, I entrust to Your divine hands all that weighs me down. Lift my eyes to Your holy face that I may see the everlasting Love for me in Your eyes. Jesus, my Brother, please help me to accept Your

Love. I shall use love and affirmation to heal my body that houses my spirit. Help me find proper rest and recreation, nourishment and nurturing. You are my Master. Please fill me with Your strength.

Violence Turned to Peace

The Advocate, the Holy Spirit that the Father
will send in my name—he will teach you
everything and remind you of all that [I] told
you. Peace I leave with you; my peace I give
to you. Not as the world gives do I give it to you.
Do not let your hearts be troubled or afraid.
John 14:26–27

Q. BLESSED MOTHER, THERE IS SO MUCH VIOLENCE AND PAIN IN THE WORLD. WHAT CAN I DO ABOUT IT? A. Pray and sacrifice for poor sinners. Do only our Father's holy Will. Your will is deceptive. Surrender yourself. Deliver yourself over to the Father for poor sinners. Be a ransom with Jesus and me.

Meditation

I have nothing to give. Everything I am and I have belongs to God. It is only illusion that I am in charge of anything except my own decisions.

Daily Application

I truly must be careful in every moment lest I grieve the Heart of God again and again by my indifference and negligence. I shall focus on the promises and commands of Christ at all times. Today, my quest is to soothe the pain I encounter, calm the agitation I meet, and be an instrument of peace and healing wherever I am.

Prayer

Dear Spiritual Mother, though I am not strong or brave, I give my entire life to you, with no reservations. I ask only that you present me to Jesus at every moment. Guard me well that I submit with great love, peace, and joy to His every desire. Please give me patient endurance to accept all that life presents to me with graciousness and total abandonment to God's holy Will. Your Divine Son changed water into the sweetest wine at your request. Please present my family, living, deceased, and yet to be born, with all our weaknesses, failures, mistakes, and triumphs to Jesus with great love. He is our Savior. In my hands these are small, yet in His hands they are much. Spiritual Mother, give Jesus my heart, all my yesterdays and tomorrows too. Please give Jesus my life swaddled in your loving embrace forever.

Angels Turned to Playmates and Confidants

[Mary] has by grace been exalted above
all angels and men.
—Second Vatican Council

Q. SPIRITUAL MOTHER, WHERE ARE THE ANGELS?
A. Jesus has surrounded me with all His angels. He desires that you use His angels as your playmates and confidants. You give the angels great pleasure when you turn to them. My angels surround you. They guard you with me. You are my beloved child. Trust me always.

Meditation

God has provided us with mighty angel power to bless us now this day and night. Is it God's perfect Will that I allow His angels, peaceful and glorious, to love and serve God's holy pleasure in us all.

Daily Application

Be still my heart and know that God is God. Idle chatter to God's angels offends His Justice. I shall speak of and to His angels with reverence. God has assigned His angels to me as friends, guides, and servants among God's people. Today, I venerate God's servants with gracious hospitality, gratitude, and awareness by reminding myself of their presence, their love, and their power. Today and everyday I search for evidence of God's angels, truly active in my life and the lives of those I love and serve.

Prayer

Dear Queen of Angels, you are forever the glory of all that is beauty and light. Spiritual Mother of all the angels, they come to you bowing and praising the divine Will of the Creator of all that is seen and not seen. Queen of Angels, my own dear Blessed Mother, what words shall I choose to speak to you? Who am I that the Mother of my Lord is my Mother? Who am I that the Queen of all the angels of God is with me now?

Thank You, dear God, for sharing Your Blessed Mother with me, for surrounding her with Your mighty angels, for allowing her to assign her holy angels to bless and light my path. Dear Lord of all the angels, son of Mary, my Brother, You alone have dominion over my reality and the reality of the whole world! Have mercy on us all. Grant us Your peace. Our human needs are Your angels' delight.

Guide us, holy angels of the Lord. Please manifest yourselves to us. Embrace us in your holiness until we dwell with you in God alone.

Chapter Six

SECRETS FROM THE DEPTHS

*I will not leave you orphans: I will come to you. In a
little while the world will no longer see me, but you will
see me, because I live and you will live. On that day
you will realize that I am in my Father and you are in me
and I in you. Whoever has my commandments and
observes them is the one who loves me. And whoever
loves me will be loved by my Father, and I will love
him and reveal myself to him.*
—John 14:18–21

From Lost to Found

*Jesus said: "Have I been with you for so long a
time and you still do not know me . . . Whoever
has seen me has seen the Father. How can you
say, 'Show us the Father?' Do you not believe
that I am in the Father and the Father is in me?"*
—John 14:9–10

Q. SPIRITUAL MOTHER, WHERE IS GOD?

A. God is always here for you, and within you and around you. Surrender unto God. Live in His abiding Love.

Meditation

I desire to love God totally and to love others as I love myself—for God, with God, and in God. It is not yet easy to love God completely, but I greatly desire to observe God's sacred commandments.

Daily Application

Today, I embrace the commandments of God as a barometer for my behavior. Each hour that I am awake, on the hour, I shall briefly investigate my behavior.

Prayer

Spiritual Mother, Jesus' Word promises that I will see Him because He lives. Jesus told us that He is in our Father and that I am in Jesus and Jesus is in me. Pray for me that I have the faith to believe your Son's Word, the knowledge to understand His Word, and the love to obey His Word. Please, Blessed Mother of Bethlehem, kiss your tiny Babe for me and for all humanity. He whom the universe and all the galaxies cannot contain or comprehend remains forever your own flesh and your blood. O divine Will of God, Humility is Your Name. Mary is truly Your own great and hidden Masterpiece. Yet You give her to me and to all who call to her. Blessed be God.

From Nothing to Everything

Whoever believes in me, as scripture says:
"Rivers of living water will flow
from within him."
—*John 7:38*

Jesus said: "[B]ut whoever drinks the water
I shall give will never thirst; the water I shall
give will become in him a spring of water
welling up to eternal life."
—*John 4:14*

Q. SPIRITUAL MOTHER, HOW DO I LIVE IN GOD?
A. God is Love. Love forgives everything. Love blesses everything. Jesus is the living water that quenches your thirst. Drink Jesus.

Q. BLESSED MOTHER, HOW DO I DRINK JESUS?
A. Drink Jesus through love. In prayer, you develop the strength to love. The more you pray, the

more you love. The more you love, the closer you are to God.

Meditation

When I walk with God, all things are possible. God carries my hurts. God carries my disappointments. My feelings die with my body. My choices live on for all eternity.

Daily Application

Today, I acknowledge my indwelling spirit's needs as each hour sounds. With the help of my Guardian Angel, I shall perform five selfless, unrecognized, and unseen acts of kindness for others today.

Prayer

Spiritual Mother, please intercede for me now to respond to every situation only with strength, wisdom, and love. Love is firm. Love is gentle. Love is always forgiving. Love is always patient. Love never tires. Love comes from God. Love leads to God. Dear God, please help me to live only in Your Love. Then will I know peace. Then will I be peace, Your peace. Dear God, allow me to love with Your Love. Jesus is God. I trust God. Trust is my badge. Trust is my avenue. My trust implies love. My love is the child of faith. Faith is God's gift to me. Prayer is my gift to God. I trust that when my faith and my prayer combine, my life in God does thrive. Dear God, the river of Love carries me to the Promised Land. The river of Love is gentleness, sweetness, peace. The river of Love flows to the Heart of God.

From Enemies to Friends

We say that the heavenly Father is the origin of everything, that everything originates from the Most Holy Trinity. We cannot see God. Jesus descended on earth to make Him known to us. The Most Blessed Virgin is the one in whom we venerate the Holy Spirit, because she is His spouse. . . . The Third Person of the Trinity did not become incarnate. Nevertheless, the expression, "Spouse of the Holy Spirit" is much more profound than mere human usage. . . . [W]e can say, in a unique sense, that the Immaculate One is the incarnation of the Holy Spirit. . . . Mary is not divine. . . . Mary and the Holy Spirit remain two distinct persons and two distinct natures.
—St. Maximilian Kolbe

Q. SPIRITUAL MOTHER, IS IT WRONG TO SPEAK TO MY FRIENDS ABOUT PEOPLE WHO IRRITATE ME?

A. Pray always to dwell in the love of the Holy Spirit. Abandon yourself totally to God. Allow yourself to belong to God. When you speak without love about another, you create unrest in yourself. You do nothing to your victim, but you allow yourself to be Satan's victim. When you speak without love, you become Satan's accomplice.

Meditation

People who know God find Him in the meek and the haughty. I too desire to find God in all His people. I shall search for God in His vast universe, and when I see His animals, trees, rivers, skies, and seas. I shall feel the effects of God's presence when the wind blows, when the snow flies and the rains come. I want to recognize God's joys, His sorrows, His rewards, and His vengeance (ST. AUGUSTINE). God is Love. God loves me as I am. He has created the earth for me and the animals, trees, rivers, the wind, the stars, and the sky. God does share His joys and His sorrows with me.

It hurts me very much in ways I cannot heal when people I treasure grow sick and cannot or will not love. It hurts too when any person (including me) is cruel, selfish, or unkind. Does God hurt when I do? I know so. There is no problem too big for God to solve. But I must ask His help, for God is Living Humility.

Daily Application

Today, I ask God's help in all my relationships. I shall wait, however long it takes, until God makes me and everyone and everything I love a beautiful new beginning to cherish forever. Today I make three sacrifices on behalf of my worst enemy.* These acts of kindness shall remain my secret with God.

Prayer

Dear Queen of Angels, please ask your spouse, the Holy Spirit of Love, to enlighten my mind to see myself as I really am. Illumine obstacles that block the flow of God's grace in my life. Show me the selfish, self-defeating behavior I undertake. Nudge me when I overestimate problems. Stop me when I underestimate my abilities. Protect me when I overestimate my capacity. Deliver

---

*Some examples: donate to the poor, renounce coffee, sugar, alcohol, tobacco, or some other non-necessity such as desserts, serve at a soup kitchen, help the elderly, do some pro bono or volunteer work, do at least one clean-up chore in a public area, or any other kindness to help someone.

me from negative or false appraisals that distort my judgment. Please ask God to help me gently accept less than perfection from myself and others, to give me a trusting and grateful heart filled with love for God's holy Will.

Spiritual Mother, bathe me in the warmth of God's gracious providence. Fill each day of my life with divine sunshine of confidence in God's power to make every moment a glorious symphony of Love, joy, and abundance.

From Spite to Compassion

The life of grace depends on the degree of nearness
of the soul to [Holy Mary] the Immaculate One.
The nearer the soul is to her, the purer it becomes,
the livelier its faith becomes, the fairer its love;
all the virtues being the work of grace,
are strengthened and vivified.
—St. Maximilian Kolbe

Q. SPIRITUAL MOTHER, WHAT AM I TO DO WHEN I EXPERIENCE THE URGE TO ACT OR SPEAK WITHOUT LOVE?
A. Be careful. Be silent. Never act toward or speak about another soul except to bless that soul.

Meditation

Who am I that I should label, and possibly libel, God's handiwork? Only God knows the secrets of our hearts. Each of His people bears beautiful treasures within themselves. God's grace alone manifests His beauty hidden in each person. These truths can heal my urges to speak (and act) without love.

Daily Application

When I have spoken without love, who have I injured? How can I make restitution today? The very least I can do is to pray for all those I have verbally or otherwise injured. God's mercy is greater than all His works. I too strive to be merciful in my thoughts, words, and deeds. Jesus makes all things and people and places new, in countless mornings of mercy, steeped in love. Thank you, Jesus. You are eternal life and Love.

Prayer

Please pray for me, Holy Mother of God, that I may be made worthy of the promises of Christ. Thank you for loving me unconditionally. Thank you for your presence, your love, and your care. Please ask Jesus to change my heart, to fill me with His Love. Show me the glories of God's power at work in all life. When I experience the urge to judge people or circumstances and events by their outward appearances, kindly send holy angels of light with the great torch of truth to refresh my judgment and calm my trembling tongue. Remind me always that God alone judges His people.

From Cruelty to Kindness

. . . [I]n all things humankind still finds rebellion. I [God the Father] did not do this for want of providence or concern for your well-being but with great providence and concern for your well-being, to take away your trust in the world and make you run straight to Me, your Goal. Thus the vexation of troubles, if nothing else, will make you raise your heart and will above the world. But people are so foolishly ignorant of the Truth and so weak when it comes to worldly pleasures that even with all these wearisome thorns they find in them they seem unwilling to rise above them, unconcerned about returning to their Homeland. . . . That is why in My Providence I allow the world to bring forth so many troubles for them, both to prove their

virtue and that I may have reason to reward
them for their suffering and the violence
they do to themselves. . . .
—*St. Catherine of Siena*

Q. SPIRITUAL MOTHER, SOMETIMES PEOPLE ARE QUITE
CRUEL TO ME. WHAT SHALL I DO?
A. Love God's children. God will correct them in
His own time and His own ways. Remember that
vengeance is His. Be patient. All will be well. Be at
peace. I always bring you peace. You are God's
child and you are my child. Come to me in all
your sorrows and disappointments. Have an orderly room when you pray. Have an orderly heart
when you pray. Pray in the silence of your heart.
Trust God's unconditional love and providence in
your life. Listen for my voice. I am your Spiritual
Mother Most Faithful. I am with you. I bring you
your Savior. His power of Love heals and restores.
Embrace the virtue of prudence.

Meditation

I did not make the world, or myself. I have
great power within me and around me to become
wise, happy, healthy, strong, and loving. That
power is God's Love for me. I must know and embrace only God's Will. Deprivation, degradation,

despair, and death, though allowed by God, do not come from God.

Daily Application

Today, on the hour, I discipline myself to pray. At each waking hour, I praise God's Love and God's mercy. I ask my Guardian Angel to sing songs of thanks to God for me at each moment of my life in time. As I praise and thank God, I shall embrace the virtue of prudence. In that light, I shall find God's Will for me today, for God wills only the best for me and all His people. I shall meet each affront with peace and offer kindness in return.

Prayer

Dear God my Father, thank You for all the opportunities You present to me each day to demonstrate my love for You. You are present in all life. Nothing happens to me that You do not allow. I choose You as my life, my commitment, and my goal. Please grant that I love You totally by wisely forgiving and loving all my enemies with no thought of return except Your holy Will be done by me. Protect me, Lord, for You alone are joy and peace and Love.

From Absence to Presence

I [God] am that Supreme Providence Who never betrays My servants' hope in Me in soul or body.
—*St. Catherine of Siena*

Q. SPIRITUAL MOTHER, YOU KNOW GOD, YOU LIVE IN GOD: WHERE ARE YOU? I NEED TO EXPERIENCE YOUR PRESENCE NOW.

A. Dear child of my heart, you belong to God. In God's providence, I am always here with you. Pray, my child. Pray now and I will pray with you. See me and hear me with the eyes and ears of faith. See me and hear me with great trust in God's promises. You will consciously know when you are with me by my peace. Where I am, the source of peace reigns. When you consciously come to me, you experience my peace. When you turn to the world and away from me, you find no peace. Do only God's Will.

Q. HOW DO I DO GOD'S WILL ALWAYS?

A. Always live in God's presence. When you experience peace, you know you are within God's Will. Trust God's providence. Trust God's hand guiding you. Suffering is transitory. Suffering, when it is part of God's Will, sanctifies. You will know your own faithfulness by the degree of your love. The fire of love in your heart extinguishes fear, doubt, and fatigue.

Meditation

Do I recognize divine peace? Do I truly desire divine peace? Divine peace is expensive: It does cost everything that is not of God, for God, with God. Do I embrace divine peace?

Daily Application

Today, should I experience agitation, I shall stop what I am doing, pray, and listen with the ears of faith to God's gentle reminder that I am over-reaching or underreaching His Plan for me.

Prayer

Queen of Angels, you who are Queen of Peace, fill my mind with words of Truth. Bring me your Blessed Spouse, the Holy Spirit, who flows forth from God the Father and God the Son. Draw me into the secret chambers of Divinity where all is silent in adoration before the one true God.

From Human Love to Divine Love

[God said] "My wealth is infinite. . . .
Everything was made by Me, and without Me
nothing can exist. Therefore, if it is beauty you
want, I am Beauty. If you want goodness, I
am Goodness, for I am supremely good. I am
Wisdom. I am kind. I am compassionate; I
am the Just and Merciful God. I am generous, not
miserly. I give to those who ask of Me, open to
those who knock in truth, and answer to those
who call out to Me. I am not ungrateful but
grateful and mindful to reward those who will toil
for Me, for the glory and praise of My name.
I am joyful, and I keep the soul who clothes
herself in my will in supreme joy."
—St. Catherine of Siena

Q. SPIRITUAL MOTHER, HOW DO I FIND AND LIVE IN
GOD'S HOLY WILL?
A. Draw nearer to me, little child of my heart. I
am a clear reflection of the Will of God. His love
and light and mercy shine through me to my children. Those who dwell with me learn the mysteries of God's divine Love and light and mercy. I
invite you now to come with me into a secret
sanctuary of Divinity. Listen to the silence. Know

that demons of despair die away and seeds of new life spring from old in silent adoration before the one true God.

Meditation

For once I see. Hello Love! You alone are Love!

At last You allow me to find You! Holy are You!

Today I hear His Voice in the singing sounds of nature.

Today I behold His Beauty in nuggets of nature that speckle His World.

Today, I see His Handiwork in every heart that lives.

Today I bless His Handiwork in every heart that loves.

Daily Application

I retire to the mountain of prayer by finding solitude at least twice today. I will not be hungry, tired, or hurried during these times. As I give God my best, He fills me with His best.

Prayer

Blessed are You, my Lord and my God. Blessed be Your holy Will. As it was in the Beginning, is now and ever shall be. Your holy Will is my bread and my water. Your holy Will is my nourishment now and forever. How beautiful are the secrets of divine Love. My God, You alone are Love. Holy Love. Holy beauty. Holy peace.

FROM TENSION TO TRANQUILLITY

God added: "This is the sign that I am giving for all ages to come, of the covenant between me and you and every living creature with you: I set my bow in the clouds to serve as a sign of the covenant between me and the earth. . . . As the bow appears in the clouds, I will see it and recall the everlasting covenant that I have established between God and all living beings—all mortal creatures that are on the earth."
—Genesis 9:12–16

Q. BLESSED MOTHER, HOW DO I MANAGE CONSTANT TENSION?
A. Stay very close to me from now on. At any provocation, always turn to me. I bring you my Son. This is the time of your visitation (LUKE 1:39–45). I am your eternal Mother.

Meditation

Do I recognize this time of my visitation?*
Scripture warns of woe to those who miss the
time of their visitation.

Daily Application

Today, moment by moment, I surrender ten-
sions and troubles to the providence of God. Today, I acknowledge that God sees everything, hears
everything, and is the Lord of reality.

Prayer

Dear God, You are my source, my goal. I sur-
render all that transpires in my life to Your loving
providence. Thank You for allowing Your Blessed
Mother to take me by the hand into Your divine
Will. Remember me kindly when I stumble, for
You are kindness. Place me gently into the caldron

---

*There is much evidence that the Blessed Mother of Jesus has been
appearing throughout history and, more particularly, in the world at
the close of the twentieth century to people of all faiths and nations.
I have written about some of the apparitions in previous books. Mary,
as she did for Elizabeth and John the Baptist in Elizabeth's womb,
brings joy, peace, and love to those who receive her. Her messages
during the last decade are disclosed as urgent pleas for reconciliation
among men by means of immediate return to the ways of God's
Love. This book is arranged so as to offer an opportunity for any sin-
cere reader to draw near to the graces of the Mother of Jesus in a
"personal visitation."

of incense that perfumes Your divine Love. You alone are holy. Blessed be God forever.

From Insecurity to Confidence

Only the person who renounces self-importance,
who no longer struggles to defend or assert himself,
can be large enough for God's boundless action.
—*St. Edith Stein*

Q. BLESSED MOTHER, WHY DO YOU BOTHER WITH ME?
A. My love for you is beyond measure. You are a unique masterpiece of God's Love. You are God's treasure, valuable beyond compare. All of paradise awaits you. All of Paradise cheers you on as you journey in the land of exile. Your life on earth is but a day. Rejoice, little child of the Kingdom of God's Love. Trust me more. I desire you to trust me totally. Be certain of my love for you in all things, in all circumstances. My love for you is eternal. It has no bounds. My love for you is God's Love. He has sent me to you. Dear little treasure of God's Heart, become living peace.

Meditation

Do I allow myself to taste God's pure Love for me? Is my faith strong enough to believe that I am God's treasure? Do I treasure these daily visits with Mary, my Spiritual Mother? Am I thankful for her presence and her wisdom that she so generously shares with me? Mary asks me to keep my heart pure. She reminds me that I belong to God alone. Mary desires me to live in the Heart of her Son for all eternity. Will I begin that process now?

Daily Application

Today, I ask Mary to help me allow God to love me as He desires. Today, I listen carefully for His Voice. I must pray more. I must spend time alone with God if I am to hear His Voice. God speaks in the silence of my heart. I must constantly prepare a place and time for God. Then I must come to God in peace. God has much to teach me. Jesus is the path of eternal life. Today, I find my path is very steep. Today, I pray with great confidence in God's presence. I want to know God and to praise God more.

Prayer

Dear God, I long to love You with no limits. May I sense Your presence now? When, like Mary,

I too am able to love all people, with no limits, and all circumstances that You allow to color the paths of my life, only then will my surrender to You be complete. Dear God, I love You. Please help my lack of love. Prod me, Lord. Lift me, Lord, to the mountain of your holy Will now. May only Your holy Will be my life. May Your perfect Plan for me be realized.

From Miserliness to Generosity

Only once do the souls understand the reason for
their purgatory: the moment in which they leave
this life. After that moment, that knowledge
disappears. Immersed in charity, incapable of
deviating from it, they can only will or desire
pure love. There is no joy save that in paradise to
be compared to the joy of the souls in purgatory.
This joy increases day by day because of the
way in which the love of God corresponds to
that of the soul, since the impediment to
that love is worn away daily.
—St. Catherine of Genoa

Q. Spiritual Mother, sometimes it is difficult for people to share. Yet, people desire peace. People desire human friendship. How can people be certain they are not being used?

A. As you come to know my Son Jesus better, you will understand the sickness of selfishness. Think of Jesus. Read His sacred Word every day. Think always about the words of Jesus. He who possesses everything carried nothing when He walked the earth. He whose power rules the world shares and shares and shares. Love my Son Jesus more. Love Him totally. Love all other things, and people, and places through Him, and with Him, and in Him. Be like Jesus. Share and share and share.

Meditation

God is mystery. God's Love transcends my understanding. God's presence in all that lives is a mystery that confounds my intellect. There are no spiritual rituals or exercises, sacrifices or gifts that influence or manipulate God. Union with God's holy Will is my only path of life. Jesus promised: "I AM." Who else has the words of everlasting life?

Daily Application

Today, I practice developing "Teflon" hands, and a "Teflon" heart. I need hands that love and serve but grasp and possess not. I need a human heart that pours out God's Love and kindness and generosity to all creation but beats only for God. I know I must give up things and people and places

I cannot keep to get what I cannot lose. Therefore, I give all I have now in His Name.

Prayer

Jesus, Son of the Living God, have mercy on me, a poor sinner. Take from me what I cannot give of myself. Fill me with Your presence, Your Love, Your peace. Jesus, You are enough for me forever.

Chapter Seven
CLEAR LIGHT

*And he [God] gave him [Jesus Christ] power and glory,
and a kingdom: and all peoples, tribes and tongues
shall serve him: his power is an everlasting
power that shall not be taken away: and his
kingdom that shall not be destroyed.*
—Daniel 7:14

From Bondage to Freedom

*That vision, which the Lord granted me, will
never leave me. I will say of it what I can and
leave the understanding of it to those for whom
God wills it. The source of all suffering is sin,
either original or actual. The soul in its creation is
pure and simple, free from all stain, and endowed
with a certain instinct for God. Original sin
weakens that instinct. Once actual sin weighs
down the soul still more, the distance between the*

> soul and God becomes greater yet; and it increases
> still more as the soul, moving even further
> away from Him, becomes evil.
> —St. Catherine of Genoa

Q. BLESSED MOTHER, I WANT TO TRULY KNOW JESUS.
PLEASE SHARE WITH ME THE MYSTERIES OF YOUR DI-
VINE SON JESUS.
A. Jesus is God. He made you. He is your Savior.
He redeemed you. He alone divinizes you. Jesus is
The Reality. Jesus frees you from bondage.

Meditation

Where does Jesus fit into my life? His mercy
and Love endure from generation to generation.
His Love unchains me from sin that holds me in
bondage to the kingdom of illusion. Love's fire
consumes non-love. How do I get the fire of love
in my heart? I live in God's presence. I must make
space in my heart for God. By an act of my will, I
unite my spirit now to God's unfathomable Love.
I leave myself in God. I lose myself in God.

Daily Application

During this time I have left on earth, I strive
to experience all God's creation as an act of praise
and gratitude. I strive to live as God's very dear
child in His Kingdom of Love. Beginning today, I

eliminate superficial, frivolous activities and give that time to prayer and works of kindness that no one sees.

Prayer

Lord Jesus Christ, Son of the Living God, please rescue me from the grips of evil. Please make my spirit pure and simple, free from all stain as it was when You created me. Please release me from trivia-seeking that evaporates Your presence in my mind's eye. Mercifully renew my spirit with a burning instinct only for God. May I never look at the sinful nature of any human. Jesus, You have freed us from bondage to sin. Jesus, You are medicine for sick souls. I run to You, Jesus, with great confidence and love and gratitude. Sin has no power to hold a blood-bought child of Yours. All power in Heaven and on earth has been given to You. Now I know why You forbade us to criticize, condemn, or judge one another. To judge one another is to eliminate You, Lord Jesus, from the world. You are the Savior of the world. You break all fetters that bind us to less than You. The judgment of one human toward another is non-truth. You alone are the way and the Truth, dear Jesus. You are life and freedom.

From Weakness to Strength

> *"She [St. Monica] strove to win him [her*
> *husband] to You [Jesus], speaking to him about*
> *You through her conduct, by which You made her*
> *beautiful, an object of reverent love, and a source*
> *of admiration to her husband. . . . She looked*
> *forward to seeing Your mercy upon him, so that*
> *he would believe in You and be made chaste. . . .*
> *[J]ust as he was remarkable for kindness, so also*
> *was he given to violent anger. However, she had*
> *learned to avoid resisting her husband when he*
> *was angry, not only by deeds but even by words."*
> —St. Augustine (writing of his
> mother and father)

Q. Blessed Mother, it requires great strength to walk the path of Jesus. I am small and weak. All humans are truly small and weak for we are totally dependent upon one another. How do I acquire great strength to follow Jesus to the Promised Land?

A. Rely always upon the Love, power, and strength of Jesus, your Brother. Walk in peace and be kindness to your family and to all those God places on your path each day. Surrender your weakness to my Son Jesus by releasing all ill thoughts, feelings, or words into His healing hands. Love your family more. Every member of your family is hand-chosen for you by God. Be patient. Be forgiving. God knows all things. God can do all things. God loves you unconditionally. Read the Scriptures for and with your family. Ponder together the ways of the Holy Family of Nazareth. Recognize strength in unity. Jesus, Joseph, and I love you. Be happy in our love and care for you. You give me great joy by praying to Joseph. Few realize his power. It is the power of Love. Those who turn to his patronage experience abundance, peace, and prosperity. Graces abound for those who understand the heart of Joseph. Protection is his gift. Turn to him always, dear child, for Jesus and I dwell with him. Those who look at Joseph see Jesus and me. So it must be for all families who live in love. Stay faithful. Never compromise. Live in our love. Share our love. Become our love. We are one family in God. Love is power. Love is strength. Love is unity. Unity is love in action. Ponder the Holy Trinity.

Meditation

Am I growing in my capacity to love, to share, and to live in peace with myself, my past, my today, and all my tomorrows? Am I willing to join my heart and hands and resources with others for the love of God? The first step toward Heaven is walked by acquiring strength to live in peace, love, and service to my family and then to others. When I am alienated from my family, I am weak and sad. God's grace unifies. God's grace brings strength out of weakness. I need God's grace. We all need God's grace.

Daily Application

Today, I pray for and perform acts of kindness that no one sees or knows about for the member of my family I least admire. I promise never to speak of this to anyone in this lifetime. I will do this for the love of God alone. God is never outdone in generosity.

Prayer

Spiritual Mother, thank you for sharing your Holy Family with me. Thank you forever for giving us your Son Jesus. May I know Joseph personally? Does he come to people when they call to him? How does Jesus respond to the pleas of Joseph on our behalf? Please pray for me, my family, and for all those I encounter that we may be like you in virtue, especially in obedience to God's holy Will. Holy Mary, Mother of God, your Holy Family is the perfect family. Please bless my family, especially the ones I find most difficult. Kindly protect every aspect of my life with the loving presence and graciousness of your Son Jesus. Please be with each of us now and at the hour of

our deaths, Holy Family, Jesus, Mary, and Joseph.
May we always imitate your perfect obedience to
God's sublime Will. Mary and Joseph, may your
love, generosity, and dedication to Jesus be our
path, our light, and our sustenance. May the unity
of your love be our strength forever.

From Worry to Serenity

*"Blessed are they who have not seen, yet have
believed" (John 20:29). Every part of nature,
from the distant stars to the tiniest flower, is a
mystery. You admit you do not understand these
natural mysteries. Do you expect then to
understand the mysteries of God? Do you expect
to see clearly the things of God when you see so
imperfectly those of earth? We must not compare
the weak powers of the human mind with the
power and mighty works of a Being Who is
infinitely beyond our comprehension. God would
no longer be God if we were able to penetrate
with mere reason the depths of His Being. To
believe what the eye does not see and the mind
does not understand is to offer perfect homage to
the Supreme Truth.*
—*Alexander Joseph de Rouville*

Q. BLESSED MOTHER, WILL YOU ALWAYS BE WITH ME IN THIS WAY? I HAVE SO MANY WORRIES AND CONCERNS THAT I DON'T KNOW IF I COULD MANAGE WITHOUT YOUR PRESENCE.

A. You are my child. I am with you. This Mother never abandons any of her children. Please pray more. Please spend more time alone with me. Your life on earth is short, like the life of a flower. Ask me fewer questions. Do not try to lead me. Be still. Listen. I desire to lead you into the Heart of God. God's serenity is yours when you love and serve one another in God and for God and with God. Obey God's Will with great trust in His Love for you. Listen carefully for the voice of God. When your will and mind and heart and longings are focused upon God alone, you dwell on the mountain of peace where none can disturb your serenity. Peace, dear child. Only peace.

Meditation

When I grow agitated, do I cling merely to the comfort zone of my intellect? There are other ways to find peace. Do I pray when worry assails my composure? I shall discipline myself to pray in all small matters so that when crises come, as they do in all lives, I surrender quickly into the providence of God's Love.

Daily Application

When I grow agitated, I shall allow God to be God by immediately surrendering all my malaise to His loving hands. I shall listen to calming music that lifts my spirit to the sublime. I shall light candles to flicker with fire that speaks to me of God's eternal Love. I shall appropriate relaxation techniques that calm my knotted body and soothe my trembling heart. I shall treasure nature and dwell in calm serenity before the mystery of God's presence. I shall hold a baby and see a man. I shall comfort an octogenarian and see an angel. I shall smell a flower and thank a snowflake. I shall sing a song and hear You, Lord God, dancing in the wind.

Prayer

Dear Spiritual Mother, Queen of Angels, teach me gentle melodies from the Kingdom of God's Love. Travel through the world and awaken once again in every spirit the memories of our true Homeland. God has placed His blessing upon us, O Blessed Mother of God. Bring us the day when humankind escapes the liar's trap that wounds each soul. Bring us Jesus now. Please ask Jesus to lift us high on the mountain of peace, O Queen of Angels, high above the liar's trap that mars the beauty of your Son's presence in our world. Thank you for remaining with us. Your perfect Mother's heart of pure love is our safe harbor.

From Apathy to Enthusiasm

*[S]peak with Him [Jesus] as with a Father, a
Brother, a Lord and a Spouse—and, sometimes
in one way and sometimes in another, He will
teach you what you must do to please Him. Do
not be foolish; ask Him to let you speak to Him,
and as He is your [Father, Brother, Lord, and]
Spouse, to treat you as His [son or daughter,
brother or sister, subject or servant, groom or]
bride. Remember how important it is for you to
have understood this truth—that the Lord is
within us and that we should be there with Him.*
—*St. Teresa of Avila*

Q. SPIRITUAL MOTHER, I CANNOT ENDURE ANOTHER
MOMENT. CERTAIN PEOPLE I MUST DEAL WITH ARE
TOTALLY INDIFFERENT, ACTUALLY UNCARING ABOUT
THINGS THAT ARE HIGHLY IMPORTANT TO ME. WHAT
CAN I DO?
A. Go to these people. You now know your true
family is the Lord and all His people. Be God's Heart
and hands to your family, your friends, your associates. You will find Jesus in your encounters. See your
family, your friends, your associates with new, caring

eyes of love. Speak fewer words and show the joy of your commitments. How you respond to each provocation determines the depths of your love. Love begets love. Sin separates. Grace unifies.

Meditation

The Lord is present in all that lives. The Lord is present within me. The Lord is Father, Son, and Holy Spirit. The Lord is my true family. The Lord is the Beginning of no beginning. The Lord is the End of no end. The Lord is my life.

Daily Application

I need to pray constantly for eyes to see God in the world, ears to hear His Voice, and a heart that beats for God alone until the divine presence and the divine gaze become my life. I need to love. Only love. Love untested is no love at all. I need to emulate sacrificial people such as Mother Teresa, Mahatma Gandhi, and Martin Luther King, Jr. I need to see Jesus in the rich and the poor, the haughty and the meek. I need to love with His Love. Only then will I be an authentic human.

Prayer

Lord, like Your Blessed Mother, allow me please to love You, to serve You, to praise You, to

know You as You are, to be for You always as You
desire me to be. Only then will I taste of the
Empyrean Spring of Living Joy. Only then will I
taste life. Allow me, Lord of life, to love for You,
in You, with You forever. Make me a living chan-
nel of Your Love. Amen.

From Misfortune to Opportunity

Jesus told her, "I am the resurrection and the life;
whoever believes in me, even if he dies, will
live, and everyone who lives and believes in
me will never die. Do you believe this?"
—John 11:25–26

Q. BLESSED MOTHER, I SEE SICKNESS AND DEATH
EVERYWHERE. VIOLENCE STALKS THE STREETS OF THE
EARTH WITH DEADLY FORCE. WHAT SHOULD I DO?
A. Dear child, your time on earth is short. Eternity is forever. Prepare for your journey to eternity. Pray. Abandon yourself to God's holy Will.
Allow yourself to belong totally to God. God
never abandons you. Give your burdens to My
Son. For Jesus your burdens are light. Jesus alone
gives you rest. Jesus has overcome the violence of
the world. Live in the Heart of Jesus. Jesus is the

only solution to all the problems of the world. Jesus is Truth. Soon everyone will recognize Truth.

Meditation

How much do I trust that Jesus is the only solution to all the problems in creation? Does my life reflect that trust? What can I do today to bring the messages of Jesus to living expression in the world?

Daily Application

Today, I imbibe the divine elixir of Jesus' Word.

Today, I live the divine elixir of Jesus' way.

Today, I step out in faith and use my hands, my assets, my time, talent, strengths, and weaknesses to actualize the presence of Christ where I am, in every situation God places before me. Whatever He asks of me, I will do. Wherever He calls me, I will go.

Prayer

Jesus, You are light and Love and peace. Dear source of peace, quickly open our eyes to Truth. Call us forth from the island of selfishness that buries the earth's progeny in caves of distortion and degradation. Come, Lord Jesus. Awaken Your people. Release our chains of death. Carry us to the mountain of God's holy Will where we cross over to the waiting arms of Our Father in Heaven. Hallowed be His Name. His Kingdom come. His Will be done on earth as it is in Heaven through You and for You and with You, Lord Jesus, forever. Amen.

From Pain to Composure

And so I saw that God rejoices that He is our Father, and God rejoices that He is our Mother, and God rejoices that He is our true spouse, and that our soul is His beloved wife. And Christ rejoices that He is our brother, and Jesus rejoices that He is our savior. . . . Christ has compassion on us because of sin. . . . I saw that every kind of compassion which one has for one's fellow in love is Christ in us.
—*Blessed Dame Julian of Norwich*

Q. BLESSED MOTHER, I HAVE MUCH PAIN IN THESE TIMES. CAN YOU HELP ME?
A. Seek only God's Will. Pray more. Sacrifice more. Simplify your life. Eliminate needless things in your life. Do not worry. Worry is lack of trust in God. Trust God totally. All will be well. Entrust your sufferings to Jesus. The child who gave my Son five loaves watched multitudes dine and receive their fill. So it is with your pain when it is

deposited in the sacred hands of Jesus.* Jesus is the Lord of health. Jesus is the Lord of wealth. Jesus is the source of peace. Jesus is living prosperity. Turn to Jesus my child.

Meditation

I trust in God's power to make all things well, including me. I am not foolishly proud to believe my pain is too great for God's power of perfection. I give my pain to Jesus now. I recognize that Jesus does work in and through the medical community.

Daily Application

Today, I entrust to the sacred hands of Jesus my pitiful pain. I do not know why I have this pain, or for whom it is intended. Lord, I give what I have, trusting that I too shall see Jesus, living health, living wealth, living prosperity, bring the miracle I now pray for by name.

---

*A small boy gave Jesus five loaves and two fishes (John 6:9–13). With this food donation, Jesus fed five thousand men and remaindered twelve baskets of leftovers. Pain upsets and often disables us. We are not divine. When we give *anything* to Jesus, He changes it into divine glory. Since our pain is of no eternal value to us where we are now, it is the height of wisdom to transfer it to the divine hands of Jesus. In His hands, our donated pain becomes ornaments of great splendor at the wedding feast of the Lamb.

Prayer

Dear God, I gratefully praise You. Thank You for Your Love and compassion. Thank You for the gift of life and love and abundance. I desire to love You, dear God, with all my heart, all my mind, all my spirit. Please help my lack of love. Please cure my lack of trust. I bless You, Lord, God of power and might. Please bless me now. Send me angels of consolation to remove the darkness that mocks my pain. Please let the light of Your divine Love warm the cold and heal the sorrow of every painful moment. Please bless my family and everyone everywhere. Please bless the earth, and the planets too. May Your holy Will be my holy will now and forever. Lord Jesus, source of peace, to You I give my life, my pain, my weakness, my poverty, my powerlessness to heal myself. Please, Lord of health, Jesus, my Brother, place Your divine hand upon me and restore me to perfect health, abundance, joy, and peace in You forever. Amen.

From Anxiety to Wisdom

Jesus said to him, "I am the way and the truth and the life. No one comes to the Father except through me."
—*John 14:6*

Q. SPIRITUAL MOTHER, HOW SHALL I PLAN FOR THE
FUTURE?
A. Surrender your plans to God's holy Will. Live
the virtues. You cannot know what is to come.
That is for God alone. Think only of His holy
Will for you now. Embrace prudence. Surrender.
Obey. Be peaceful. Rest in God's holy Will. Rec-
ognize God's immense Love for you in everything.
Be peace, dear child of my heart. Only peace.

Meditation

Little children know they can control little.
Wise people know they can control nothing.

Daily Application

Today, when anxiety assaults me, I will stop,
breathe in God's Love, slowly exhale my gratitude,
and remember I am not in control. God is and I
trust Him completely.

Prayer

Lamb of God, You take away the sins of the
world. Have mercy on us. Spare us, O Lord. Jesus,
Son of the Living God, grant us peace. Amen.

Chapter Eight

SOLUTIONS FROM THE MOUNTAIN

There shall be no harm or ruin on all my holy mountain;
for the earth shall be filled with knowledge of
the LORD, as water covers the sea.
—Isaiah 11:9

FROM CONFUSION TO UNDERSTANDING

The special motives for which St. Joseph has been
proclaimed Patron of the Church . . . are that
Joseph was the spouse of Mary and that he was
reputed the father of Jesus Christ. From these
sources have sprung his dignity, his holiness, his
glory. In truth, the dignity of the Mother of God
is so lofty that naught created can rank above it.
But as Joseph has been united to the Blessed
Virgin by the ties of marriage, it may not be

doubted that he approached nearer than any to
the eminent dignity by which the Mother of God
surpasses so nobly all created natures. For
marriage is the most intimate of all unions, which
from its essence imparts a community of gifts
between those joined together by it. Thus, in
giving Joseph the Blessed Virgin as spouse, God
appointed him to be, not only her life's
companion . . . but also, by virtue of the
marriage, a participator in her sublime dignity.
—*Pope Leo XIII*

Q. BLESSED MOTHER, WHY DO I FIND IT SO UNPLEAS-
ANT WHEN MY SPOUSE, MY CHILD, MY RELATIVES, OR
OTHERS I LOVE MISUNDERSTAND ME?

A. No creature can give you the love you seek.
Your heart is wounded with a longing for the divine. Your suffering is to be without that fullness
now. Go now and love and serve others to honor
God. Be constant in your love for God as God is
constant in His love for you. Love others for the
love of God. Expect no recompense from people.
God is enough for you. Pray that I might enter
into the hearts of all God's children. As I enter
their hearts, I prepare a place for my Son to dwell.
Come now, dear child, into my Immaculate
Heart. There you find the treasures of God He has
allowed my children.

Meditation

Those who seek love, fame, and glory for themselves are robbers (DEUTERONOMY 6:4–5). All honor and glory and power belong to God. I must love all that is and was and will be for God, with God, in God. Such detachment is difficult. We cannot find fulfillment in and through humans, though our longings would tell us differently. Greedy demands for human love, affirmation, and respect rear up and lead and deceive us until we acquire the hard-won freedom of detachment. Detachment is a sweet alliance of my heart exclusively with the Heart of God. This is God's Will for the human race (DEUTERONOMY 5:1–33).

Daily Application

Today I carry a blessed item* on my person in a constantly noticeable way as a reminder to seek only God's Will. I actively choose to love and serve others as my response to God's sovereignty over creation. Today, I seek first the Kingdom of Heaven by consciously passing on all accolades, honors, compliments, and achievements I receive to God, their

---

*This can be something as simple as a blessed medal, a rosary, or another reminder of God's presence in the world. It is best that the "reminder of the sacred" be for the wearer's eyes only.

rightful owner. Today, I choose to remain humble and hidden, for these are God's ways. Jesus is my leader. I listen for His voice. I strive to obey His voice. The only true misunderstanding is to miss the voice of God's Will.

Prayer

Joseph of Nazareth, even you had to learn God's ways in the world. You knew human misunderstanding well. Your newborn Son, though He is God who created all that is and was and ever will be, had no home on earth at birth. None would offer Him hospitality. Though you suffered and worked to provide better, Jesus was born in the lowest estate by the design of God's holy Will so that all may approach Him. Powerful Joseph, you are the human guard of the Holy Virgin of Bethlehem. You are the human protector of her Divine Christ Child. Who gains entrance to the divine nativity but by your leave? Obedient Joseph, you responded to the angels' commands with great love. Bless your holy obedience. In you the Divine Babe and His lowly Mother found shelter. Loving Joseph, we too seek shelter in your holy love. Be our protector in the storms of rejection and exile. Remain always our father most faithful as we climb the torturous paths on the mountain of God's holy Will. Pray for us that the Mother of Jesus, whom you know best of all, may

enter into our hearts as she entered yours, and prepare there a place for her Divine Son to dwell forever.

DAILY PRAYER TO THE MOST LOVING
FATHER, SAINT JOSEPH

O Saint Joseph, whose protection is so great,
so strong, so prompt before the Throne of God,
I place in you all my interests and desires.
O Saint Joseph, do assist me by your powerful
intercession and obtain for me from the Christ
Child whom you love so uniquely, all spiritual
blessings through Jesus Christ Our Lord.
O Saint Joseph, having engaged here on earth
your heavenly power, may I offer my
thanksgiving and homage to you, the most
loving of fathers.
O Saint Joseph, I never grow weary of
contemplating you and Jesus asleep in your arms.
I dare not approach Him while He reposes near
your heart. Please embrace Him in my name and
kiss His fine Head for me, and kindly ask Him to
return the kiss when I draw my dying breath.
O Saint Jospeh, patron of departing spirits, pray
for us. Amen.

From Servant to Heir

*But when the fullness of time had come, God sent
his Son, born of a woman, born under the law, to
ransom those under the law, so that we might
receive adoption. As proof that you are children,
God sent the Spirit of his Son into our hearts,
crying out, "Abba, Father!" So you are no
longer a slave but a child, and if a child then
also an heir, through God.*
—Galatians 4:4–7

Q. SPIRITUAL MOTHER, WHY MUST I BLESS AND SERVE
OTHERS TO HONOR GOD?

A. God alone is the fullness you seek. God dwells
in all His children of the earth. Serve others to
honor God who dwells within them. God is never
outdone in generosity. Honor God your Father, for
He honors you day and night. Nothing of the earth
but God will satisfy you. Seek no rewards from
creatures. Blessed are you when you serve others in
God's holy Name to honor Him. Come to Jesus
when you feel the need for human love. You always
find Jesus in the less fortunate. He is hidden there
waiting to love you and affirm you as you relieve
His misery. Jesus left His blessing on those who
crucified Him so that it would come back to you
when you are scorned and mocked. Be like Jesus.
Rejoice in God's Love. Bless and serve God's cre-

ation. Then you will be blessed and served. Live in peace. Never fear. God's Love is stronger than all the evil in the world. Live in His Love. I give you my blessings, dear child of my heart. You too must bless others if you would be like Jesus.

Meditation

The life of Jesus is my life's pattern. Jesus is the human reality.

Daily Application

Today, I begin anew to learn the words of Jesus by reading Scripture and allow His ways to fill my longings. I shall pray before, during, and after reading Scripture.

Prayer

Blessed be God. Blessed be God's holy Will in my life. Blessed be all God's creation. Lord Jesus, open my heart and mind to know You in Spirit and Truth.

From Tears to Laughter

Amen, amen I say to you, no slave is greater
than his master nor any messenger greater
than the one who sent him. If you understand
this, blessed are you if you do it.
—John 13:16–17

Q. BLESSED MOTHER, ON DAYS WHEN IT IS DIFFICULT
TO EVEN SMILE, HOW CAN I BLESS AND SERVE OTHERS TO
HONOR GOD?

A. Dear child, please become sensitive to the
fallen humanity of others. Pray for everyone. Forgive all as God forgives you. Then you will be
forgiven. Give your life totally to God. Hold nothing back. God alone can fill you. God alone can
give you the strength to love. When you are weary,
turn to me. Please pray with me. Allow me to enfold you in my heart. My heart is filled with God's
Love. Dwell always in the chalice of God's Will
where every tear turns to joy. Be careful, my child,
of the voices you hear. Temptation is strong for
all my children in these times. The voices of the
world constantly beckon my children to ways that
distort truth. See television as a great possibility
for good. In these times some voices speak to my
children from the television screen that are not
pure. Those who listen bring into their conscious-

ness sights, ideas, and sounds that lead my dear little ones on the path of perdition. Abstain from voices that are not pure. Peace, dear child. Do not fear. The victory belongs to my Son. It is the virtue of trust in God's Word that protects my children. Be a vigilant disciple of Truth. Cling to Truth. You know where to find Truth. Jesus is Truth.

Meditation

God gives rain and sorrow and want, and He gives peace and joy and Love. This is God's world. I never offend God when I turn to Him in love. Jesus says a repentant heart is God's great treasure. If Jesus is God, then His Word, His example, His ways are Truth. If Jesus is God, it is the highest wisdom to become His faithful disciple forever. I need strong faith to live the belief that Jesus is God. I need strong trust in God's Word to follow Jesus. I need strong love to live like Jesus for Jesus.

Daily Application

I strive today to be a vigilant disciple of Truth. I will cheerfully seek joy and peace and confidence as tools that change pain and sorrow to love. I work today to honor God in harmony with His Plan for His children. Today, I look for God in the marketplace. I embrace peace, trusting that God does provide. I look for God in the eyes and appetites of His children. I look for God in His world of commerce as He feeds the lost sheep of the House of Israel. I seek God's blessing as He moves among us. I thank God who bumps me and prods me and pushes me.

Prayer

O blessed Faith, fill my mind and heart and will.

O blessed Hope, allow me to hope against all hope.

O blessed Love, Holy is Your Name. Jesus is Love. Jesus is God. Blessed be the Name of Jesus, King and forever Lord of my heart. Blessed be Jesus, the Way and the Truth and the Life. Blessed be the paths of God forever!

From Sickness to Health

If you love me, you will keep my commandments.
And I will ask the Father, and he will give you
another Advocate to be with you always, the Spirit
of truth, which the world cannot accept, because it
neither sees nor knows it. But you know it,
because it remains with you, and will be in you.
—John 14:15–17

Q. SPIRITUAL MOTHER, QUEEN OF ANGELS, WHY ARE YOU GIVING MESSAGES NOW LIKE NEVER BEFORE IN HISTORY?

A. Moral sickness plagues the world. I am speaking to my children now as never before in history through the love and mercy of my Divine Son Jesus.

Q. SPIRITUAL MOTHER, QUEEN OF ANGELS, WHAT DOES JESUS WANT US TO DO WITH YOUR MESSAGES?

A. Jesus wants you to listen carefully and live my messages. He gives you my guidance to point you into the Heart of God. Please surrender totally to God's holy Will in all things. Share my life with you and my messages by your example. God alone is Love. In all situations of your life, be totally confident of God's eternal Love for you. Allow Jesus to fill you with the healing power of the Holy Spirit of Love. God alone is Truth. Live Truth, my child. Be Truth. Truth is God's healing presence. God never leaves you. God alone is Love. His Love is not bounded by the earth. Love God more. Pray always. Trust always. God is Order. Your life is confusing to you when you do not turn to God, for you are God's child. He made you for Himself. God requires faithfulness in all circumstances. Entrust to God all your painful confusion. God heals and restores all His children who turn to Him. Surrender to God's Love, dear child of my heart. Allow God to love you into wholeness.

Q. How do I do this, dear Blessed Mother?

A. Pray always with great confidence in God's Love for you. Ask with faith and trust, and you shall receive. You do not see me now, for I am with you in peace and faith and hope. My Son is Lord of the Cosmos. I, His Mother, am Queen of the Cosmos. See me always with eyes of hope. Trust me always in deep faith. The gift of faith from God our Father is your treasure as you walk the path of earth. Love, my child. Always love. When your heart is filled with love, you have no space for fear, anger, envy, jealousy, lust, division, greed, avarice, or malevolence. A heart filled with love is the resting place of the Holy Trinity. Such a heart is the treasure of the Holy Trinity. It is in prayer, united to obedience to God's work, God's Will, that my children are capable of love. My Son is Love. I am the Mother of Love. Cling to me, dear child. Cling to my love. My love is strength. My love is union with God.

Meditation

To live, I need the Holy Spirit of Truth, I need the Holy Spirit of Love, I need the Holy Spirit of Order. All people need Truth, Love, and Order. Each of us desperately needs Divine Wisdom, Understanding, Council, Knowledge, Fortitude, Piety, and Fear of the Lord.

Daily Application

Today, I pray with renewed fervor for a deeper awareness and a refreshing outpouring of the gifts of the Holy Spirit to lead me to the Throne of the Holy Trinity.

Prayer

Dear Spiritual Mother, please ask Jesus to send upon us His precious gift of the indwelling Holy Spirit. Your Divine Son, Jesus our Brother, sits at the right hand of our Father. Please obtain His divine blessing for me and for all people on earth. I do want to be healed. I want to be well. I want my heart to be God's dwelling place. Thank you, dear Mother Most Faithful, for praying with me, for teaching me to recognize Truth. Guide each of us on the earth to the unfathomable chambers of Divinity where peace is life and joy is food and Love is rivers of living splendor that echo in the Heart of God and delight His children with cherished oneness forever.

From Separation to Union

Do not work for food that perishes but for the food that endures for eternal life, which the Son of

Man will give you.
For on him the Father, God, has set his seal.
—*John 6:27*

Q. SPIRITUAL MOTHER, WHY DO I INADVERTENTLY
SEPARATE MYSELF FROM GOD'S LOVE, AND HUMAN LOVE
TOO?
A. Pray always for the gift of wisdom. Choose
wisely at all times. Seek forgiveness in all your failings. God never withholds forgiveness to those
who seek. Trust God's promises to you. You alone
have the power to refuse God's Love. No creature
can separate you from God's Love but you.

Q. BLESSED MOTHER, WE DO SEPARATE OURSELVES
FROM GOD, BUT WHY?
A. God helps you if you allow God to influence
your decisions. God desires integrity of heart. God
desires peace in His children's hearts. There is no
peace where God is not. God departs from those
who disregard their responsibilities to Him and to
one another.

Q. WHAT A HORRIBLE PUNISHMENT, DEAR BLESSED
MOTHER.
A. See the fisherman in high seas. He has no nav-
igation tools but God. Those who survive the
times of storm in their lives are those who use
every talent they possess with great responsibility

and cry to God at every moment from the depths of their hearts.

Allow my life to be your pattern. I am the lowly one. I am the Mother of the only-begotten of the Father. His Will is done, dear child, in lowliness. His Will is done in absolute obedience. Obedience to the Will of God is meekness. Be meek as I am meek, my child. Seek lowliness. Seek silence, for in silence the Will of our Father is discovered.

The ways of the world bring greed, violence, and war. The ways of God bring abundance, peace, and generous love. Be aware, dear child. Our Father does reward a thousand fold. The evil one detests the generosity of our Father. Live in truth, dear little one of my heart. Practice obedience.

Meditation

Am I my own worst enemy? Do I drive God and His protection away by carelessly disregarding my responsibilities to Him and to others? Do I truly desire to surrender my life to the divine power of God's unconditional Love for me and all His creation? Do I plead always for the gift of wisdom? Do I have a humble and contrite heart?

Daily Application

Today, I guard every thought, word, and deed flowing from me. Let nothing I think, say, or do grieve the Heart of God, or separate me from recognition of His divine presence in me, around me, and always looking at me. Let me serve His children, His creation, and all that He allows to cross my path this day with deep reverence, love, and gratitude.

Prayer

Dear God, my Father, in Jesus' name, allow me the joy of knowing the power of Your Love and the joy of Your presence. Let the light of Your Love increase in my conscious awareness as each moment of my life unfolds before You. May the glory of Your Kingdom reign in my heart, my family, my work, my country, and in the world. May my burdens, in the hands of Jesus, turn to gossamer wings that carry me swiftly along the currents of Your mercy to the garden of Your divine beauty and tranquillity. May Your eternal Kingdom of joy reign in me in sublime splendor forever.

Jesus, King of my heart, lift me into Your Heart. Jesus, King of my heart, carry me in Your Heart to our Father forever. Bless me, Lord of the angels, illumine Your Kingdom. Free me to live in

Your Heart, O Son of God and son of Mary. Jesus, source of peace, Lord of the angels, king and center of the universe, my Brother, all praise, honor, and glory be Yours now and forever. Jesus, my Love, my eternal Paradise, Jesus, my source, awaken me to life in You forever.

From Grudges to Forgiveness

Then Jesus said, "Father, forgive them, they
know not what they do."
—Luke 23:34

Q. BLESSED MOTHER, WHY IS IT SO DIFFICULT FOR US TO SINCERELY FORGIVE ONE ANOTHER?
A. Sin is strong. A proud person does not forgive. A proud person does not seek forgiveness. To be like Jesus, you must forgive. Always remember that if you are not like Jesus you will be unable to find Him to choose Him. You are my child. Trust my path. It leads you to God's Will for you.

Often God allows circumstances to test and try His faithful children. It is in response to my children's actions that the Kingdom of God on earth is built. Come, my child. Come to my Mother's heart. I am the Mother of life in God. I am a refuge. I am a shelter. I am the place of abandonment to God's Will. Those who love God know me well. They experience my tenderness. They experience my power.

Trust my Son's Love for me. His Love for me is a sign of His Love for you and for all my children. Jesus is life in God. Those who know me know God well. See God's mercy for the whole world. Wars, ethnic cleansing, concentration camps are the ways of mankind without God. There has always been injustice in the world. Jesus is God. Even Jesus, God in human form, suffered the injustice of men without God. His compassion is enough for all people of all time. His forgiveness is the healing balm of love for all people. His mercy is the conduit through which God's Love flows to a sinful world. It is only through God's mercy that the depravity of hatred is transfixed into the wounds of Jesus. Jesus is Love. Jesus is mercy. Jesus is forgiveness. Jesus is eternal life for all God's children. Those who cling to Him never die. They live on in His merciful Love for all eternity as I do. Peace, dear child. Peace in the Sacred Heart of Jesus, for peace is the merciful Heart of Jesus.

Meditation

Forgiveness is the sublime affirmation of God's power to make all things well. To forgive is to trust God. If I refuse to forgive, I hold others to a higher standard than does God. When I forgive others, I am truly free.

Daily Application

Today, I pray to forgive with my whole heart, my whole mind, and my entire will. I will practice this prayer constantly by my attitude and my behavior.

Prayer

Dear Lord Jesus Christ my Savior, Lord of all creation, pour the grace of Your Precious Blood upon my heart of stone. Free me, Lord, of the darkness that binds me blind to Your presence. Melt all lack of forgiveness that lingers in me and petrifies my feeble attempts to love. Lord Jesus, please heal me. Make me holy. Give me the spirit of Mary. Fill me with her virtues, for she is the delight of Your Heart. Your apostles received that gift for themselves and all the Church. Your Heart and Your Mother's Heart are one, O Lord Jesus, my God. We long for abiding awareness of Your presence among us. Come, Lord Jesus. Awaken us now.

From Sadness to Happiness

[T]he Archangel Gabriel was sent to the Virgin.
When she gave her consent to him, the Holy
Spirit came upon her like a divine fire inflaming
her soul and sanctifying her flesh in perfect purity.
She endured such fire by the power of the Most
High that overshadowed her. By the action of that
power, instantly His [Jesus'] body was formed,
His soul created, and at once both were united to
the Divinity in the Person of the Son, so that the
same Person was God and man, with the
properties of each nature maintained.
—*St. Bonaventure*

Q. SPIRITUAL MOTHER, QUEEN OF ANGELS, PLEASE
TELL ME HOW TO BE VERY HAPPY TODAY.

A. Help your family, all your brothers and sisters,
your relatives, your acquaintances, and everyone
you encounter to be like Jesus by your example.
Pray. Persevere. I am here for you with my Divine
Son. Turn to Jesus always. Never look away, even
for a moment. Jesus is happiness. Live with Jesus.
Happiness begets happiness. Trust God. Be happy
in His promises. Make God first in your life. Jesus
is God. Jesus is holiness. All holiness comes from
Jesus. Holiness is life in Jesus. His Heart sighs and
pines to fill the longings of God's children. Jesus

alone is the fulfillment all people of the earth crave. Come into His Heart, dear little ones. Know His tenderness. Know His compassion. Seek Jesus. He brings all the joys of life, for Jesus is life. Jesus is beauty. Jesus is peace.

Meditation

Do I truly know God's promises to the human race? Do I trust those promises? My happiness is rooted in God, my Creator, Savior, Sanctifier. God made me. God knows me. God loves me. God's promises are my happiness.

Daily Application

I decide today to become lovingly familiar with the ways of God. Silence is God's way. I shall dine often today on silence. Silence is God's Plan. I shall fill my life's free moments by learning the great spiritual classics, attending conferences and seminars that illumine God's ways, seeking people, places, and things that are consecrated to God's Will.

Prayer

Spiritual Mother, take my poor heart and press it to your own heart so rich with virtue. Fill

my heart with your joy, for you see God, you know God, you belong totally to God. Stay near me, dear Mother of God. Hold me firm until I grow strong enough to stand with Jesus in meekness and obedient love that destroy my disgrace.*
Awaken me gently, dear Mother, to the presence of the source of peace in the sacred sanctuaries of divinity forever.

From Ignorance to Knowledge

*While . . . [Saint] Francis [of Assisi] was living
in the church of the Virgin Mother of God,
he prayed to her who had conceived the Word
full of grace and truth, imploring her with
continuous sighs to become his advocate.
Through the merits of the Mother of Mercy,
he conceived and brought to birth
the spirit of the truth of the Gospel.*
—St. Bonaventure

Q. SPIRITUAL MOTHER, QUEEN OF ANGELS, WILL YOU TEACH ME YOUR WISDOM?

---

*Meekness and obedience will unite us to Christ. He is living meekness and obedient Love. Meekness and obedient Love act as an antidote that destroys the disgrace we inherit from original sin.

A. God's Will must be your will in all things. Think only of God's Will before you make any decision. Trust God in all circumstances. Please honor your Father, O children of the world. Honor His children. Honor His choices. Honor His ways. Honor His Heart.

Meditation

Do I recognize God's Will in my life, moment by moment and decision by decision?

When I experience peace, I know I am within God's Will for me.

Daily Application

I surrender moment by moment to indwelling peace by holding fast to the hand of Mary, my Spiritual Mother Most Loving. I do this by steeping my agenda in her ways of humility, meekness, and gentleness. I will assert myself only when God's justice so demands. I will drink deep of the gifts God communicates to me in the isolation of prayer. I will clear my mind and heart of all that is not of God, for God, and with God in order to give Him bountiful hospitality there.

Prayer

Dear Mother of God, my Spiritual Mother, help me to honor God in every one of His people. Grant me grace to respond to the slightest hint of His pleasure at all times, in all places, in all circumstances.

Dear Queen of Heaven and earth, build towers of crystal faith that gleam in my reality. Construct a palace of hope for me to share. Give me eyes that see God's Love in all that lives: in birds and flowers and forests and streams, in the old and the helpless, the young and impetuous, in market places that bustle and fill human needs, in concert halls that fill human dreams, in rain and sunshine, in the cold and the heat, in all things bright and sweet, and in all that is dark and sad and bleak.

Take me with you into the Heart of God forever.

From Deviancy to Decency

I knew nothing of evil, so I was afraid to meet it. I had not yet found out that nothing can be unclean for those who have clean hearts, and that a simple virtuous soul sees evil in nothing, for evil exists not in things, but in corrupt hearts.
—St. Therese of Lisieux

Q. Spiritual Mother, Queen of Angels, how can
I love God with my whole heart and others too
while evil exists everywhere?
A. Keep your heart pure.

Q. What does that mean?
A. Keep your heart clean.

Q. How do I keep my heart clean?
A. Dear child, a clean heart beats for God alone.
Keep your heart for God alone. Never give your
heart to anyone else. See everything and everyone
in your life in relationship to your faithfulness to
God. Keep God first. Keep God as your goal, your
source, your life, your only love. Keep your heart
clean.

Q. Dear Spiritual Mother, what exactly is a
clean heart?
A. A clean heart is detached from all that is not
God. See all things through God, and in God, and
with God. Be still. Be silent. See God in every circumstance of your life. Be one with God through
Jesus in the Blessed Sacrament.

Meditation

Time with God and significant others enables
me to love and to grow. God's time transforms the
world. I am created in God's image and likeness,

and so is everyone else. My highest thoughts flow from consciousness of my God-like powers (JOHN 14:11–14). I need a pure heart. As I think, so I feel and behave. What I do not talk out, I may well act out. My tongue is a barometer of the condition of my heart. As it speaks, so my heart is diagnosed. Talking with God, my Spiritual Mother Mary, and those I love is life-giving. I am as tender and open to newness as I am forgiven my trespasses.

The place to learn trust in forgiveness of all my trespasses is before the Blessed Sacrament in Eucharistic Adoration. Once I am calm before the Blessed Sacrament, I experience deep healing and spiritual growth. Courage grows in me. Moral choices are clearer. Relativism decreases. Christ loves me unconditionally. Love bears responsibility. He is Eucharistically present among us.

We each *need* to love one another unconditionally, but we are repelled by ungodlike behavior in ourselves and others. My Spiritual Mother shows me that my spiritual life is rooted in the humility of self-confidence. Her life experiences help me realize that the higher God raises us, the more humble our self.

Daily Application

To grow in decency and flee evil, I come to Jesus, my Eucharistic Lord in the Blessed Sacrament each day.* The humility I gain each day before the Blessed Sacrament allows me never to try to be more than I am and never to try to be less than I am. This grounds me in truth. True humility teaches me to work to be the "I am" that I am, and sacrifice to be the "I am" that I can be. True humility illumines that my life is meant to be a feast, not a famine. My life on earth is meant to allow me to be a victor, not a victim. In front of the Blessed Sacrament each day, I acquire strength never to let anyone put me down. In front of the Blessed Sacrament each day, I am bathed in the truth that God eternally cherishes me. In front of the Blessed Sacrament each day, I receive the courage to give God permission over me so that I can become all God wants me to become.

Prayer

Dear Mother of the Eucharistic Christ, those who draw near His Presence in the Blessed Sacra-

*Eucharistic Adoration of the Blessed Sacrament is offered daily in many churches, chapels, monasteries, convents, residences, and public buildings throughout the world. For example, in New York City, at St. Patrick's Cathedral, in Washington, D.C., at the Basilica Shrine of the Immaculate Conception, in Bethesda, MD, at Our Lady of Lourdes Church, in Scottsdale, AZ, at St. Maria Garetti Church, in Pittsburgh, PA, at St. Mary of the Point Church, in London at Westminster Abbey, in Sussex at Worth Abbey. The purpose of Eucharistic adoration is to communicate spirit to Spirit with Jesus Christ truly present in the Blessed Sacrament via transubstantiation.

ment come at your invitation. I hear you calling to all of us:

O children of my heart, come to the Lamb.

Come to His Heart. Come to His ways.

Come to your Father, o little children of mine.

I bring peace. I bring joy. I bring hope.

I bring solutions to the cruelty of pride.

I bring Love.

My children, God is Love. My Son is God.

My Son longs for you.

See my lonely Child. See my suffering Child.

See my own Child waiting and hoping and loving.

Come to Him, o my children, that He may give you Love and life.

Come and abide with Him daily in the Blessed Sacrament.

From Aloofness to Intimacy

It is in Heaven that we shall know our titles
of nobility. Then each of us will receive his
due reward from God. The first, the most noble,
and the richest will be he who on earth
chose to be the poorest and the least
known for the love of Our Lord.
—St. Therese of Lisieux

Q. Spiritual Mother, why is every human relationship laced with suffering?

A. You are looking for God in relationships. No
human being can fulfill your thirst for love. Focus
only on Truth. You must develop eyes to look at
God in each relationship. Love God who dwells
within your relationships. Only then will your relationships be pure. Any other form of love is dis-
guised self-love, rooted in the earth-bound ego.
Self-love is life-sapping. True love is life-giving.
Try more diligently to see God everywhere. You
know God never leaves you. Please acknowledge
Him. Speak to God. Listen to God. Obey God.

Meditation

God made the world. God sustains everything.
God nurtures everything. I am not separate from
God. No creature on earth can live without God's
sustenance. No relationship is blessed that is not for
God, with God, and in God. God dwells in all that
lives. I am His eternal treasure. I can distance myself
from the truth of who I most deeply am by ignor-
ing God's presence within me, around me, and in
me as I cling to just the material world I see, touch,
taste, smell, and feel while forgetting to appreciate
the deeper meaning behind all visible reality. I can
build a fable out of my life on earth and play the
leading role. The jaws of death will draw down the
curtain on my mere self-centered life, and then I

will be alone with God at last. How good God is. His name is True Love. I choose True Love now.

Daily Application

From now on, I pray to see myself as God sees me. I pray to cherish myself as God cherishes me. From now on, I look for God, truly present in every situation, event, and person in my life. I listen to God with ears of faith. I will to love God with total trust in His power to make me and every person, place, and thing in my life a beautiful mosaic of His true love forever.

Prayer

I can do nothing without you, Lord.

Help me to find Your ways in all my thoughts, words, and deeds, and especially in my relationships with people.

Change my heart of stone into Your garden of Paradise.

Plant anew in me the tree of eternal life for You alone.

Lord, that I might believe as You desire.

Lord, that I might trust as You require.

Lord, that I might love as You inspire.

*F*ROM *D*ESIRE TO *F*ULFILLMENT

I wait for you, O Lord; I lift up my soul to my
God. In you I trust; do not let me be disgraced;
do not let my enemies gloat over me.
—*Psalm 25:1–2*

Q. SPIRITUAL MOTHER, QUEEN OF ANGELS, WHY IS
GOD INTERESTED IN EVERY DETAIL OF MY LIFE?
A. You belong to God. He desires you to desire
Him in your life in every decision you make. Hear
His Voice. You must fast, my child. Fast that the evil
one have no power over you. Choose a day and take
no solid food until three P.M. The hour of divine
mercy (three P.M.) is a harbor for the world. Honor
that time. Always honor that time. Feel the wound
in my Son's Heart at three P.M. Share His loneliness
and longing. I am the Mother of Divine Mercy.

Meditation

Jesus prayed. Jesus fasted. I, His servant, am no
greater than my Master. I therefore must pray and
fast as Jesus did.

Daily Application

I choose to fast. I shall fast today as you ask.

Prayer

Spiritual Mother of Mercy, true Queen of Angels, pray for me, pray for all people on earth that we bend our wills to your loving guidance now. Please pray with me now. Show me God's perfect Will for me today.

From Absence to Presence

Now with you is Wisdom, who knows your works and was present when you made the world; who understands what is pleasing in your eyes and what is comfortable with your commands.
—*Wisdom 9:9*

Q. SPIRITUAL MOTHER, IS GOD EVER TOO BUSY TO BE INVOLVED IN HUMAN MINUTIAE?

A. Dear child, please awaken to Truth. God is never too busy for the slightest detail of your life. God sees everything. God knows everything. He redeemed you with His own blood. He loves you beyond your capacity now to understand. God loves all His children, especially the lost ones. Re-

member my words well, dear child. Prayer and
fasting can change the natural law and human law
too. Pray and fast that I might help you. Now is the
time. Come, little ones. Enter into your Spiritual
Mother's heart. There you are safe. There you belong to the Redeemer.

Meditation

In the Sacred Heart of Jesus, each of us becomes children of our Father. Jesus paid an enor-
mous price for us. Our Father patiently awaits all
His little ones of the earth.

Daily Application

Today, when I am weary and feel alienated and
absent from God's presence in the world, I look at
a crucifix and it unmasks the folly of mere worldly
wisdom. Jesus died on a cross. That historical fact illumines much I need to know today about the lie
of eternal absence. I know Jesus is not dead. Today,
looking at the crucifix, I see my life united with
millions of people who have seen Jesus, spoken
with Him, eaten with Him, walked with Him,
served with Him, and died for Him since his historical crucifixion two thousand years ago. I fast
now from mere worldly vision. With eyes of faith
and trust, I see Jesus here with me today. Jesus and
His Mother Mary see me now, at this moment.

They are opening their hearts to me. Today, my faith and love show me the presence of my eternal family.

Prayer

I desire to claim my inheritance, dear Father. In Jesus' Name, please receive me now.

From Lost to Found

The LORD begot me, the firstborn of his ways,
the forerunner of his prodigies of long ago.
—Proverbs 8:22

Q. Spiritual Mother, who are God's lost children?
A. They are His children who have not yet tasted the sweetness of His presence in their lives. Please help them as I have helped you. Show them God's Love by your life, by your choices. Give them hope. Speak to them about God's mercy. Tell them of God's immense, unfathomable Love for all His children. No one is excluded from this love. The presence of the Blessed Sacrament on earth is a great blessing and an eternal treasure. The souls of those who come into the presence of the Blessed Sacrament are enriched with divine grace. Soon the

whole world will be on fire with the presence of the Blessed Sacrament. Soon all people will be bathed in the divine grace of the Blessed Sacrament. It is then that Jesus' word shall live in the hearts of God's children. Those who know God realize the folly of man's decisions without the light of divine grace. Live in stillness. My Son comes when you least expect Him. Will you be awaiting Him? Those who are busy about the things and ideas of the world miss His visitation. They weep and wail but they find Him not. Call to Him day and night. Look for Him everywhere, in every circumstance of your life. Those who seek Him find Him. He longs to be found.

Meditation

The angelic message "Do not fear. Peace on earth to men of good will" echoes now throughout the land. Warriors for good are peace-keepers. If God is with us, what need is there to fear?

Daily Application

Do I truly desire Jesus as the Lord of my life? Does fear seep into my days and nights, unnoticed until it claims my peace and forces me to hide from truth? I release all fear into the sacred hands of Jesus, my Savior.

Prayer

Spiritual Mother, Queen of Angels, filled with God's Love and grace, please clothe me with your virtue. Let the light of your glories shine through me to all God's people. Bind me to you, o Holy Mother of God, and bring me to Jesus in great love, great peace, and great joy. Your Son is leading His flock away from arid soil where chicanery reigns, to fertile soil rich with His bounty. Help me never to miss the time of my visitation.

Chapter Nine
APPROACHING GOD

By advancing and progressing "from glory to glory,"
the light of the Trinity will shine in
ever more brilliant rays.
—*St. Gregory of Nazianzus*

RECOGNIZING GOD

I [Jesus] have given to everyone a golden tube of
such power that he may draw whatever he desires
from the infinite depths of my divine heart.
—*St. Gertrude of Helfta*

Q. SPIRITUAL MOTHER, QUEEN OF ANGELS, WHAT
IS THE MOST PLEASING WAY THAT I MIGHT APPROACH
GOD?
A. God's children do not grovel before Him. He
made all His children to be one with Him. God is

the light of each human soul. God commands us to live in His Love always. It is God's pleasure that you approach His presence with Jesus and me. Come to me all you little children of God. Be assured that I judge no one. I am the faithful Mother. I have all the rewards of the earth with which to bless my children. Those who turn to me in confidence and obedience never want. I walk with Jesus. The Heart of Jesus and my heart are one. Dear little child of the Kingdom of Heaven, enter into that Kingdom now. The Kingdom of Heaven is within. Accept the kingship of my Divine Son Jesus. Jesus is Lord of the Cosmos. His children are royalty by His blood. Be my children, little ones. I am Queen of Heaven. I am queen of earth. Be my children, for I am Queen of the Cosmos. Praise the Holy Trinity, dear little ones. He who is mighty has done great things for us and holy is His name. Blessed are you, dear little ones of my heart, for I am the Mother of God and Mother of each of you who comes to me. Allow me to bring you to my Son Jesus.

Meditation

Am I ready to approach God at this time? Am I adequately prepared to travel the path God has ordained for me from all eternity? Do I accept the Queen of Angels as my guide to the Heart of

God's Love? Do I accept her as my Spiritual
Mother who brings me to the Heart of her Son
Jesus forever?

Daily Application

Commitment to follow Jesus' way is a great
grace. I seek that grace. He promised those who
seek, find.

Prayer

Here I am, Spiritual Mother and Queen of
Angels. I place my hand in yours now. Please present me to Jesus as His loving disciple forever.

Here I am, Lord. I come to do Your holy Will.
You alone are the Lord. You alone are the Most
High. I am all Yours. Please accept my heart, Lord,
offered to You in the pure hands of Your Blessed
Mother, Queen of my heart. Lord Jesus, I believe
You, I trust You, I adore You, I love You forever.
Keep me always as Your own.

Thank you, Queen of Angels, for bringing
me to Jesus in this most treasured familial intimacy.

Thank you Jesus, my Brother, for Your
Mother and mine.

Recognizing Freedom

Blessed are they who are persecuted for the sake of
righteousness, for theirs is the kingdom of heaven.
—*Matthew 5:10*

Q. Spiritual Mother, where is personal spiritual freedom when racial, ethnic, and gender bias are rampant on earth? No area of the world is exempt from violence of all kinds. Yet we are all God's people.

A. Be vigilant. Always pray for God's help. Stay in God's Will. Only love shall set you free. Love. Only love shall set the people of the world free.

My Son guards my children with great compassion. He is the Savior of all my children's weaknesses. Those who lose their trust in His ways suffer endlessly. My Son is the Savior of all God's children who turn to Him. It is the Will of our Father that His children love and serve one another. Those who love, know peace. They experience great joy. Thank you for your attempts to trust. Our Father rewards a generous heart but never a foolish heart. Be at peace. Pray fervently. Love with a heart filled with trust.

God wants you in Heaven, but not yet. First you must complete your journey on the earth. He has covenanted with you to give you freedom to choose His ways. Those who do not choose God's ways grieve my heart.

Thank you for comforting my wounded heart. I long for all God's little children to dance before my Divine Son. I long for our Father's children to be one family in God.

I long for the female children of our Father to know peace and justice and equality. The freedom of my Son Jesus has embraced the women of your times as never before in history. Help my daughters to grow in love and trust. Come to me, little daughters. Come to the Mother of God that she may bless your femininity with the gift of divine Love.

Bring God's gifts to all His people. Help everyone, beautifully dressed in exquisite costumes, to dance and sing with tambourines and other musical instruments for Jesus, who walks among you. Never are the children of our Father meant to languish in pain and hunger and non-love. You are my children. Jesus has given His life for you that we might be one family living in our Father's Kingdom of Love and peace and joy. People of all races and ethnic backgrounds are beautiful. Dance and sing, for Jesus is among you. Jesus dances and sings with little children. How He loves my children! His skin is like yours. His ethnic background matches yours too. I sit among you. My skin is like yours. My ethnic background is like yours. We are one family, Jesus and you and I. We are one.

Allow me to thank you for your kindness to me with immense graciousness, tenderness, gratitude, and great love. Please perform a beautiful, disciplined dance for me. Where I am, so also is Jesus. Allow Jesus to touch you with immense gentleness, dear children of the world. How Jesus longs for you to recognize Him. All races and nationalities join as family in this gift to our Father. How beautiful God has made you. As Jesus is recognized and loved, there will be no sickness or deformity or hatred. In Jesus, we live in a Kingdom of peace and joy and love where all are well. All are capable. All are loved, and they know it. All have enough. All are cared for and care for one another.

Where Jesus reigns, God's earth is once again His house of prayer and His children are one.

Call to the Immaculate Heart of Mary to receive Jesus.

Jesus is divine food. Jesus is divine life. Jesus is everlasting life. Jesus is everlasting fullness. Jesus is the Way and the Truth and the Life. Jesus is the divine power of justice steeped in Love. Jesus is in the world. Jesus is the solution.

Meditation

Do I enter into racial, ethnic, and gender bias in any way? What can I do today to eradicate all human bias? How do I contribute to poisoning the environment of God's creation?

Daily Application

I shall help those who cross my path, especially the elderly, women, children, minorities, and those who are powerless. Each day, I will find someone to assist, but who it is shall be my secret forever. With God's help, I will awaken to the secrets of the earth and the environment and take care.

Prayer

Dear Spiritual Mother, Queen of Angels, I desire to be one with your Immaculate Heart at every moment. You have shined the light of God's Will from your loving heart into the darkness of my indifference on this long journey from exile to the Promised Land. Please illumine Jesus in my life. Jesus is the only Truth. Jesus is the only Life. I will try always to obey His Will. I shall pray and work to end bigotry, gender bias, cruelty, and indifference in me, around me, and from me. I praise God's justice. I bow before God's Will. Lead me forward into the Heart of God forever. The Promised Land is in God, with God, and one with God forever.

ℛecognizing ℭhoices

*Do not think that I have come to abolish the law
or the prophets. I have come not to abolish but to
fulfill. Amen, I say to you, until heaven and
earth pass away, not the smallest letter or the
smallest part of a letter will pass from the law,
until all things have taken place. Therefore,
whoever breaks one of the least of these
commandments and teaches others to do so will be
called least in the kingdom of heaven. But
whoever obeys and teaches these commandments
will be called greatest in the kingdom of heaven.*
—Matthew 5:17–19

Q. SPIRITUAL MOTHER, QUEEN OF ANGELS, HOW DO
WE ALWAYS CHOOSE GOD'S WAYS?

A. Only those who pray always are able to discern
God's ways. Those who always choose God's ways
live in peace, joy, and abiding love. Anyone who
claims to love God must obey His commandments
and ordinances with great love and commitment.
You must know God's commandments and His
ordinances to be faithful to their protection. Ask
your family to accept the kingship of my Divine
Son Jesus. Jesus is Lord of Creation. His children
are royalty by His blood. Be faithful to Jesus, my
little children. Jesus obeyed His Father perfectly.
Be like Jesus. Live Jesus' way, His truth, His life.

Q. WHAT DOES IT MEAN, DEAR BLESSED MOTHER, TO
BE SELFLESS?

A. It means, dear child, to love God above all
things He has created, including yourself. To love
that way, my child, you must know God well.
Those who pray much know God. See the elderly
in these times as God's gentle gift to the world.
Their weakness and confusion present an opportunity for each of you to experience the generosity you yourselves crave from the Eternal Father as
you grope in darkness and confusion to find God's
Will in your lives. As you share your joy and
strength and love with the elderly, God's joy and
light and Love fall upon you. That is the reason for
the majesty of the Fourth Commandment (DEU-
TERONOMY 5:16) my beloved Jesus shows to all
the world through me, and through the crucifixion. See the crucifixion as a symbol of life in Paradise, through and with and in the Fourth
Commandment. It was in obedience and love and
joy that your brother Jesus ascended the mountain
of obedience and honor to put on the garment of
immolation that brings eternal life to all God's
children (LUKE 22:42).

Be good and faithful children, dear little ones
of my heart. Be like Jesus. Difficult times fall upon
the entire population of the earth. Those who pay
homage to the god of selfishness feed off the
starving corpses of the small, the disenfranchised,
and the elderly. Children fare better, for there is

global legislation that helps children all over the earth. The light of Christ's Love is the only refuge for dark, difficult times that embrace all my children in the land of exile. Turn to Jesus, dear children. Be like Jesus. Be His Love to the world.

Meditation

Jesus is the Good Shepherd. I am called to be like Jesus in all things. Good shepherds care for their flocks. A sheep that does not respond to the voice of the shepherd is in mortal danger of being devoured by predators. The great God of Abraham, Isaac, and Jacob, Our Father, sent us Jesus the Good Shepherd. His sheep listen for His voice. Do I hear His voice? Am I faithful to His voice? Do I obey His voice? The world needs Jesus now as never before. The Good Shepherd brings His sheep to the Promised Land of our Father. Jesus is the Faithful One. He calls to everyone. His sheep dine on the splendors of our Father. Peace is their name. Love is their essence. Do I know God's word? Do I follow the Good Shepherd's way and His Truth? Am I a good shepherd of all God's people, places, and things?

Daily Application

Today, I choose joy amid the treasures of God's providence as I listen for the voice of the Good

Shepherd. Cheerfulness is my banner as I embrace service to the small, the disenfranchised, and the elderly. Today, I prayerfully choose how to share my time, my energy, and my assets with the less fortunate. God expects no less of me. I recognize this commitment as God's gift to me and with me moment by moment. I give God complete sovereignty over me, my life, my time, my desires, and possessions. In that way, I embrace Truth, for God is Lord of everything but my free will. I surrender today to God with loving trust in His ways (JOHN 14:6).

Prayer

Spiritual Mother, Queen of Angels, we cherish the wisdom you share. Forever we choose to belong to your Divine Son Jesus, our Brother, the Good Shepherd sent by our Father to lead us Home. Show us the proper way to please Him, to serve Him, to honor Him.

Give me grace, please, dear Mother of divine grace, to carve out time each hour to pray, moment by moment, to look at God, to praise God, to love God, to be one with God by serving His creation.

We pledge ourselves to remain forever your little children. Bless you, dear Mother of Jesus. We honor you as our Mother Most Faithful. We are totally yours forever. Please lead us deeply into the Heart of your Divine Son, Jesus our Savior. We wish to remain with Jesus forever. Jesus is our safety. Jesus is our life.

Jesus, our Good Shepherd, may we graze in peace within the safety of Your flock forever.

$\mathcal{R}$ECOGNIZING $\mathcal{E}$VIL

For I am convinced that neither death, nor life,
nor angels, nor principalities, nor present things,
nor future things, nor powers, nor height, nor
depth, nor any other creature will be able
to separate us from the love of God
in Christ Jesus our Lord.
—Romans 8:38–39

Q. SPIRITUAL MOTHER, QUEEN OF ANGELS, THERE IS MUCH BRUTALITY ON EARTH: WARS, DOMESTIC VIOLENCE, KILLINGS. PEOPLE DIE OF HUNGER, DISEASE, NEGLECT. WHY DOES GOD ALLOW ALL THIS HORROR?

A. It is never God's Will that His people choose evil. It is through God's Love that all His children are free to choose their behavior. The freedom of God's children to choose blessings or curses at every moment is His gift. Regardless of what the eye beholds, God's Will prevails. God's Will is done. Nothing happens that God does not allow. You are my beloved child. I guard you tenderly with my angels. Please pray for the gift of peace, dear child. Please surrender to God's Will. I am Queen of Angels, dear child. My love is constant. I am the Mother of God. I care for His children as my own. Do you not see me yet in the world, dear child? I am always beside you. Speak to me often, dear child, in the quiet of your heart. Praise my little Son, for He loves you beyond your capacity to comprehend now. He longs for your love. He longs for your joy and trust in His divine presence with you. Please allow Him to lead you to safety. There is safety only in His ways. All else is illusion. There will be peace in the world, a peace the world has never known. More of my children are becoming aware of my presence in the world. As they find me, they discover the power of Jesus' presence in the world. Pray with great gratitude for God's immense Love for you. Always trust my presence. I am your faithful Mother Most Loving.

Meditation

God never abandons any of His children. We abandon God, and He must allow us that possibility because He loves us. It is the highest wisdom to trust God's presence in my life, to rely upon His divine power and providence. I have no personal power to overcome my unseen enemies. God's presence directs me to the Promised Land. Jesus is here to lead me to safety. His shoulders are broad enough for me. Only Jesus' arms are all-powerful.

Daily Application

I am finished with needless suffering. I trust God's providence. The path of Jesus does not tolerate violence against any person. Wars, domestic injury and neglect, and killing are not God's ways. I will not enter into these aberrations in our society. I will work to eradicate these painful signs of societal deviation from truth.

Prayer

Jesus, come and rescue us, all of us throughout the world. Jesus, Prince of peace and Love, fill us with Your ways. Jesus, Lord of Creation, bless us, free us, reign in us. Praised be Jesus now and forever.

Recognizing Divine Intimacy

Seek the Lord, all you humble of the earth, who have observed his law; seek justice, seek humility; perhaps you may be sheltered on the day of the Lord's anger.
—*Zephaniah 2:3*

Q. SPIRITUAL MOTHER, QUEEN OF ANGELS, DOES
GOD KNOW EACH OF US PERSONALLY?
A. Yes, my child. God knows every hair on your
head. God knows every thought in your mind. He is
aware of every desire of your heart and every word
you speak. God alone knows each human heart.

Q. SPIRITUAL MOTHER, QUEEN OF ANGELS, DOES
GOD LOVE US, EVEN WHEN WE DISOBEY HIM?
A. God's love for each of His children is un-
changing. It is you who run away from God in
your disobedience. The Eternal Father awaits His
children. A humble and contrite heart He never
spurns. Praise the Holy Trinity, dear little ones. He
who is mighty has done great things for us and
Holy is His Name. Blessed are you, dear little ones
of my heart, for I am Mother of God and Mother
of each of you who come to me. Call to my Son.
Love my Son. Obey my Son. Be like my Son.

Meditation

Am I willing to call to Jesus today? Do I truly
love Jesus? Will I prove my love by obedience to
His commands? Am I willing and ready to be like
Jesus?

Daily Application

Today, and every day of my life, I will to imitate the life of Christ in my thoughts, words, and deeds.

Prayer

Come, Lord Jesus, King of my heart. Come, Lord Jesus, King of all Your Mother's children. Bless us, Lord of the angels. Lift us into Your Kingdom. Free us to live in Your Heart, O Son of God and son of Holy Mary. Jesus, source of peace, Lord of the angels, King of the Universe, my Brother, all praise and honor and glory be Yours, now and forever.

Jesus, King of my heart, carry me to our Father.

Jesus, King of my heart, lift me into Your Heart.

Jesus, my Brother, give me life, Jesus, my Brother, eternal life.

Jesus, my Lord, my God, my all, give me Paradise with You. Jesus, my Brother, give me You forever.

RECOGNIZING DIVINE HUGS AND KISSES

> . . . *Where has your lover gone that we may seek*
> *him with you? My lover has come down to his*
> *garden, to the beds of spice, to browse in the*
> *garden and to gather lilies. My lover belongs to me*
> *and I to him; he browses among the lilies.*
> —*Song of Songs 6:1–3*

Q. SPIRITUAL MOTHER, QUEEN OF ANGELS, HOW DO
WE KNOW AND LOVE OUR CREATOR, THE ETERNAL
FATHER?

A. Love God our Father through Jesus. Jesus told
us: "The Father and I are one." Jesus is the way to
the Eternal Father. The world is His. It exists by
His permission. All we have is through His permission. All we have is through Him. All we have
is His, as we are His. The Eucharistic presence of
Jesus enlightens the world. See the spinning sun*
as the sign of the Eucharistic presence of God in
the world. The spinning sun is a sign of God's
presence in the world making all things new. See

---

*The subjective phenomenon of the spinning sun was first observed
by approximately 75,000 people at Fatima, Portugal, in 1917, during
an apparition of the Blessed Virgin Mary to three shepherd children.
Recently, people all over the world report this recurring phenomena,
and most especially at reported Marian apparition sites and Marian
conferences.

golden rosaries* as the Christian link of God's charity in the world. See the prayer groups as God's families feeding the world on the nourishment of prayer. Prayer accesses the mysteries of God's Love in the world. Pray much, my little ones, that you might enjoy the reality of God's hugs and kisses.

Meditation

Everyone who lives is my brother and sister in Christ. We are the family of God. When I love Jesus, I love our Eternal Father in Heaven.

Daily Application

I will to open my heart this day and allow God's divine love to penetrate into every fiber of my being. I actively seek to experience God's hugs and kisses.

Prayer

Jesus, my God, You are our secret love. We look for you in the sunrise and sunset of every dream. We look for you in the glistening snow of frozen human love that beguiles and lures and mocks and exhausts the longings that drive our

---

*This phenomenon involves a mysterious changing of the chain of a rosary from a silver color to a golden color.

search for You. Jesus, You alone are our love. We dance to the tune of harsh overlords who promise rewards that rust and burst and pollute and contaminate the pristine clarity of Your presence in our secrets. Carry us to the garden of beauty, O Love. There we gaze upon the depths where roses sing and lilies dance. Come for us quickly, for we send our sigh and laugh and cry that You may be enclosed in the intensity of our expectations. We place our lips upon the morning dew that ascends to You in the noontime sun and enfold ourselves in joyful abandonment to Your holy Will forever.

Recognizing Divine Assignments

Mother of God, how often in the last centuries
have you not come down to us, speaking to us in
our mountains and groves and hills, and telling
us what was to come upon us, and we have
not heard you. How long shall we continue
to be deaf to your voice, and run our heads
into the jaws of the hell that abhors us?
—*Thomas Merton*

Q. SPIRITUAL MOTHER, QUEEN OF ANGELS, WHAT DOES GOD EXPECT OF US IN THE WORLD?
A. God commands His children to obey His perfect Will. You must be a faithful steward.

Q. SPIRITUAL MOTHER, WHAT IS A FAITHFUL STEW-
ARD?

A. A faithful steward frees himself from dependence on creatures. A faithful steward uses all created things in God, for God, and with God. A
faithful steward obeys the great commandments
and ordinances of our Father, even to the most
minute detail, out of love for God's Will.

The winds of peace are blowing over the
earth now. You shall witness a triumph of God's
glory as never before in history. The sacrifices of
my faithful children are great. Their dignity is a
sign to the world of God's beauty. No human
tragedy can contaminate God's beauty. No human
tragedy can nullify the dignity of each human soul
created by our Father, redeemed by my Son, and
sanctified by the Holy Spirit of Love.

I, God's human Mother and Mother of the
human race, your Queen of Angels, now call
upon my faithful sons and daughters throughout
the world to speak out against violence, against
tyranny, against oppression of any kind. Go to the
highways and byways of the earth. Awaken my
faithful children. Ask my faithful children to serve
God our Father with love, gratitude, and enthusiasm. End racial bigotry. End ethnic bigotry. End
gender bias. Eliminate poverty. Eliminate disease.
Eliminate all hatred that begets violence. Eliminate
selfishness that deprives others of their dignity.

Where prayer reigns, love reigns. Where prayer is absent, hatred breeds violence that chokes off the life-giving light of love, peace, and joy.

Meditation

We long to fly beyond the sunset of all that is profane to find our secret love everpresent right here within our deepest memories. When rainbows grow in the sky, do we think of life where no one cries, and no one ever dies? The perfume of the swirling winds invites me to trust the brilliance of God's mysterious Plan for His people. Can I hope for more?

Daily Application

If today I hear His Voice, I will not harden my heart, regardless of the cost. If He calls me to action today, I will respond with enthusiasm. I will use everything I have to bring the Kingdom of God's Love to life.

Prayer

Spiritual Mother, Queen of Angels, although it seems impossible to obey God perfectly, we fly unto you, O Virgin of Virgins our Mother. To you do we come, wounded and sorrowful. Carry us quickly in your heart to your Divine Son Jesus, who brings us forgiveness of all transgressions. We need to be renewed, to be washed clean in the Blood of your Lamb.

Spiritual Mother, Queen of Angels, you disclose to us God's desires for our earth journey to His Heart. Teach us to walk only His roads of earth in joyful gratitude that calls to His Heart of Love in that hiding place where mortals melt into the unfathomable mystery of His divinity.

Queen of Angels, may the assignment you have announced for our times from the Heart of God truly be realized now among all the peoples of this earth as we awaken to our relationship in the family of God.

Recognizing Divine Knowledge

Resplendent and unfading is Wisdom, and she is readily perceived by those who love her, and found by those who seek her. She hastens to make herself known in anticipation of men's desire. He who watches for her at dawn shall not be disappointed, for he shall find her sitting by his gate. For taking thought of her is the perfection of prudence, and he who for her sake keeps vigil shall quickly be free from care; because she makes her own rounds, seeking those worthy of her, and graciously appears to them in the ways, and meets them with all solitude.
—*Wisdom 6:12–16*

Q. SPIRITUAL MOTHER, WILL I BE ABLE TO FULFILL YOUR CALL? QUEEN OF ANGELS, PLEASE SING TO ME OF GOD'S HOLY MYSTERIES TO GIVE ME STRENGTH FOR THE DIVINE ASSIGNMENT YOU BRING TO ALL PEOPLE NOW.

A. My love is God's Love, dear child of the Covenant. The Mighty One has called me forth as He broods over the earth. My name is Wisdom. I sit at the foot of the throne of the Trinity with all my children. We are the sweetmeat of God's Love and His unfathomable generosity. I am His daughter, dear child. I am His love. I am His wisdom. I am His Mother. I am the house of the Lord. Bear the Light of God's Love as your Banner. Begin now to gather the peoples of the earth. We are one family in God.

The harvest is ripe. My workers are in the vineyards. Rejoice. Enjoy the power of the resurrection of my Son Jesus. He is your hope. He is your strength. He is the path to Paradise. Treasure is the name Jesus. Beauty is the name Jesus. Joy of all joy is the name Jesus. The heavens and the earth pass away but His name is. Jesus is God. Jesus is Love. Jesus is eternal life. Cling now to Jesus. Cling to His words. Cling to His ways. Cling to His Church. Dwell always in His Heart. Jesus' Heart and mine are one. Jesus' Heart and mine are your shelter. Sing with love. Join your song to the angelic choirs that comfort the Heart of God throughout the earth. Strengthen your love for

God by working with the angelic choirs for the salvation of the world. Think of the multitudes who do not know my Son Jesus, though they hear His Name and read His words. Think of the multitudes who know not even His name. Sing for the whole world, O children of our Father. Sing with the angelic choir of peace. Praise the Holy Trinity. Praise the Will of God.

Meditation

What words can I speak? God knows my heart. His grace makes all things new, even me, and His earth, His holy house of prayer, and His entire peoples of the Covenant He made with our Father Abraham. *His Will is my only life.*

Daily Application

I embrace sincerity when I pray to God. I *now* pray about everything. I say yes to God. I *shall* do only God's Will. I join my heart and voice to the angelic choir of peace. God's Will alone is the abundant life. *His Will alone is reality.*

Prayer

Dear God, most gracious Eternal Father, how can we thank you? You are our love. You are our life. You are our dreams, our longings, our goals.

You are our every moment, for You have made us from nothing yet You call us to dwell with You in Paradise.

O divine Love! Precious Father, may we be Your little children of eternal gratitude? May we dance and sing the thought You long to see and hear? May we present a gift to You, O divine Love? Alas. A gift we have not, for all is Yours, O divine Love! Here we are, Father. We come to do Your Will. That alone is the gift You seek.

Our Father, Your great gift to us, Jesus, is now our path, our hope, our life. With Him, we shall go to the highways and byways in Your holy Name, one thought and one step at a time. We choose to obey with love and joy Your divine assignment from the heart of Mary, Queen of Angels and Spiritual Mother of the human race.

Recognizing Divine Obedience

Consider your own calling, brothers. Not many of you were wise by human standards, not many were powerful, not many were of noble birth. Rather, God chose the foolish of the world to shame the wise, and God chose the weak of the world to shame the strong, and God chose the lowly and despised of the world, those who count for nothing, so that no human being might boast before God.
—1 Corinthians 1:26–29

Q. SPIRITUAL MOTHER, QUEEN OF ANGELS, WE HAVE SOUGHT TO OBEY GOD'S WILL EVEN TO THE MOST MINUTE DETAIL. YOU TAUGHT US TO OBEY GOD IN SMALL THINGS, FOR WHEN WE ARE STRONG IN SMALL THINGS, BIG THINGS WILL BE POSSIBLE. YOU HELP US FORM THE HABIT OF OBEYING GOD WITHOUT QUESTION IN EVERYTHING. DEAR SPIRITUAL MOTHER, PLEASE HELP US TO LOVE GOD ABOVE ALL THE THINGS HE HAS CREATED. TO LOVE THAT WAY, DEAR QUEEN OF ANGELS, WE MUST KNOW GOD WELL. YOU HAVE EXPLAINED THAT ONLY THOSE WHO PRAY MUCH KNOW HIM. I DO NOT YET FULLY UNDERSTAND THIS PATH OF LOVE YOU TEACH. CAN YOU HELP ME?

A. My child, often it is only in extreme suffering, loneliness, and isolation that human beings come to understand God. God is Spirit. God is Truth. Those of you who are fortunate enough to have the Eucharist in these times enjoy the bounty of God as did those who lived around my Son, Jesus, in the thirty-three years of His life on earth. In these times, few know the Eucharistic Jesus. Rest in Jesus. Jesus remains physically present with you on earth in the Eucharist. Jesus is powerful enough to solve all the needs of everyone on earth. In God's great mercy, Jesus is here for all those who long for God. I do not answer idle questions that humans must pray to understand. I do not give solutions. All solutions are centered in the gift of free will with which God our Father has endowed each of you. Know that my Son hears all prayer. My

Son answers all prayers. Turn to my Son. There you find Truth.

Meditation

God is the only reality. There is no life apart from God. God is the only Truth. God alone is our Father. God alone is our Savior. God alone is our Sanctifier. God made me. God loves me. There is no other Truth for me.

Daily Application

Only Truth is my friend. I choose not to accept non-truth, not for anyone or for anything. I am the child of Truth. To enter into Truth, I need to recognize Truth. Today, I will find Jesus, my Eucharistic Lord. He knows all things. I need to communicate spirit to Spirit with Jesus in His Eucharistic presence. I need great faith to walk this path. I pray for supernatural faith.

Prayer

Holy are You, O Eternal Father. Blessed are You, O Eternal Father. Glory and praise and thanksgiving to You, O precious, most beloved, most cherished Eternal Father. May Your Kingdom come now in my heart. May only Your Will be done in my life, always for Your greatest honor, Your pleasure, and Your eternal joy.

Recognizing Divine Victory

To accept the Gospel's demands means to affirm all of our humanity, to see it in the beauty desired by God, while at the same time recognizing, in light of the power of God Himself, our weaknesses: "What is impossible for men is possible for God" (Luke 18:27).
—*Pope John Paul II*

Q. Spiritual Mother, Queen of Angels, why is a wrong moral choice (sin) so terrible?
A. Sin hurts God because it hurts you so much. Sin separates you from God's providential care. Turn to Jesus at every moment. Jesus is always here for you. Jesus never leaves you. Jesus is your Savior. Jesus brings victory out of defeat. Come little ones into my Immaculate Heart. I am with you in a most special presence in these times. Our Father is blessing you with many rewards, for He appreciates faithfulness. All your sacrifices are very great gifts that bless my name in the world. Those who honor their Spiritual Mother are the treasures of God's providence. Persevere, dear little children,

for Jesus comes soon. Pray to Jesus, little children of my heart. Run and play. He has much to teach you in these days. Find Him in the quiet of your heart. He is everywhere that you go. The cosmos cannot contain Him. Jesus is Heaven.

Meditation

When I forget who God is, I turn from God's omnipresence and become intoxicated once again on the bitter wine of self-love. My Spiritual Mother is teaching me to recognize my life on the earth as a time to be formed into a vessel of divine love.

Daily Application

Today, I guard my actions carefully so that my choices are morally upright.

Today, I harness my thoughts so that each one is morally upright.

Today, I honor my indwelling spirit with strong moral leadership.

Today, I reaffirm that only God's Will is life.

Prayer

Dear Jesus, when I am lost and cannot find my way, You come to me in my dreams, my work, my recreation, and in my relationships and hardships and mistakes. You hunt me across the valleys and up the mountains of this earth You have made from nothing. There is no place to hide from Your gaze. You carry me when I am sick from the poison of illusion that mocks my mutinous will. You heal me again and again with each gentle beat of Your Sacred Heart of pure Love.

Thank you, Lord Jesus, for Your unconditional Love for me. Thank you for pursuing me when I run from you. Jesus, meek and humble, change my rubber heart that stretches and constricts to demands of appetites I cannot yet control, into an enduring flame of love for You that ever so slowly consumes all my artificial loves.

Truth. O beautiful Truth! Your Name is Jesus. Come, Lord Jesus. Come into the ashes of my burned-out heart and resurrect there Your citadel of eternal Love. Remind me always, Lord Jesus, that dependence upon, and addiction to mere human love of any kind prevents me from walking with God. Remind me always, Lord Jesus, that the purpose of all my relationships with people, places, or things is to deepen my capacity to give and to receive Your Love.

I now know that once the lesson is learned, You remove the object of my human affection. O how painful! Yet in You all love lives. In You there is no pain.

I hear You calling me to deeper levels of consciousness of Your divine presence in all that lives. Will I love Your creatures far more passionately now, yet with much greater detachment? Give me new loves, dear Love, only to deepen my capacity to give Your Love and receive Your Love.

Nothing is lost.
All lives forever in You.
No more loss. No more tears.
You alone, O God, are eternal life.
You alone, O God, are eternal Love.

Recognizing Divine Peace

For a child is born to us, a son is given us;
upon his shoulder dominion rests.
They name him Wonder-Counselor, God-Hero,
Father-Forever, Prince of Peace. His dominion
is vast and forever peaceful. . . .
—Isaiah 9:5–6

Q. Do you know who my secret love is, dear Queen of Angels, my Spiritual Mother?
A. Yes, my child. I know. My Son Jesus is God. God alone is your secret love. You bear an eternal wound that draws you ever onward toward the Heart of the Holy Trinity. Not until you walk with the Triune God will your heart be filled. When you walk with God, you are one with all creation, in God, with God, and for God.

Q. Spiritual Mother, is it possible to walk with God now before I pass through the portal of death?

A. That is His perfect Will, my child. You must choose to walk with God. To make that choice, you must know God well. You will always know God by His peace and His Love. You must have a clean heart to walk with God. A clean heart lives for God alone. A clean heart bends and sways to the rhythm of God's presence in cadences of intricacy that ascend and transcend the limits of human capacity and burst into the miracle of divinity. Obedience to the Will of God is your path of peace. Those who walk with God are clothed in obedience.

Dear children of the world, many of you climb to the path of God's Will by mortification. Those of you who are unable to perform voluntary mortification are aided by our loving Father in Heaven. It is through mortification of the senses that mankind is able to experience the spirit world. The corporeal, material world is a very small part of God's Plan for each child of His.

You must develop a heart that is capable of discerning Truth. Ponder my words to you that you might begin to know Truth. Struggle relentlessly to obey me. The disease of self-righteousness is healed by awareness of the plank in your own eye. You may take nothing with you, my child, but your obedience to God's Will. All else is illusion. All else is death.

The time to laugh comes. Soon the weeping will end. Peace. Only peace, dear little children. Soon all God's children shall recognize their Spiritual Mother. When they know their own Mother, they shall have their identity. When God's children know who they are, their hearts will melt into mine. Together we shall dwell before the Trinity, for holy is His Name and holy are His ways. We are one, dear little children of my Immaculate Heart.

You are my beloved children. I guard you tenderly with my angels. Please pray for the gift of peace. Please surrender to God's Will, dear children. I will never leave you. My Son Jesus is with you always. When you are one with Jesus, by the power of the Holy Spirit of Love, You shall walk with God forever.

Meditation

I am dust. It is God's Love that gives me life. Wisdom leads me to be one with Jesus, to love as He loves, to serve as He serves, to obey our Father as He obeys. God's cosmic laws are signs of His obedience. To be obedient is to be like God. God's great commandments are gifts of His divine Love. They are huge barriers to vice. Love brings peace.

Love is the path to joy. Love is the river that flows
to paradise.

Daily Application

Each day is a new occasion to surrender into
the reality of God's Love. Each day is my opportunity to choose life or death. I choose life: I choose
Jesus who is Life.

Prayer

Your arms are outstretched,
O Eternal Father of Love.
You await our arrival.
Come, Lord Jesus. Come, Prince of Peace.
Carry us to the Promised Land truly present
here beyond the rainbows
in the deepest depths of Divinity,
where we walk with God
as it was in the beginning
of no beginning,
is now and shall be forever.
Come, Lord Jesus.
Come and reclaim Your Kingdom.
Come, Lord Jesus.
Reign in my heart, my mind, my soul.
Come, Lord Jesus. Reclaim Your Kingdom.
You alone are the Lord.

You alone are the Most High.
Here I am, Lord. I await you.
Here I am, Lord. I am all Yours.
Take me, Lord.
Accept my heart, Lord,
in the hands of Your Holy Mother,
the Queen of my heart.
Peace, peace, only peace, Lord.
Your peace in my heart,
Your peace in my family,
Your peace in my world.
Come, Lord Jesus. Reign in my heart.
Come, Lord Jesus. Reclaim Your Kingdom.
Here I am, Lord, King of my heart.
Here I am, Lord, awaiting your return.
Come, Lord Jesus, King of my heart
Take us to our Father who art in Heaven.
Hallowed be His name. His Kingdom come.
His Will be be done now and forever. Amen.

Epilogue

Dear children, you are my angels.
Rest securely in my Immaculate Heart.
There you rest in my Divine Son Jesus.
I am Queen of Angels.

I am your Lady of the Earth.
I am hovering over my lands.
I wear white as a sign of my faithfulness
to all God's children.
I am eternally young.
I wear the innocence of God's Perfection
to be
Eternal Youth.
Crimson is my sash, for I weep and sigh over each
of
God's fallen children of the earth.
These lands are strewn with the blood of innocence
that
rises like incense before the Throne of God.

Hear me calling to you, O children of the earth.
Hear me in the winds that sweep across my lands
and trees and grasses and flowers.
Hear me in the bleats of cattle that
mourn with me
at the cruelty of God's children to one another.

I am your Lady of the Earth.
I am your Perfect Mother,
for I am Mother of God.
I am Mother of Innocence,
for I am Mother Most Innocent.

Grasp my sash of crimson, little ones.
Allow me to wash you in the Blood of my Lamb.
Those who sleep in my shadow
shall rise out of the ground and
sing to the Trinity like clear bells
in
the dawn of new life.

A New Heaven descends upon a renewed earth,
my children.
Listen to the sound of the bells.
Hear me in the winds of change
that
announce the presence of my Lamb
in
all that lives.

Pray, little ones.
Pray with me now.
Sing to my Lamb, little ones.
Sing and dance and praise our Father who art in
Heaven.
Do you see Him now, my little ones?

Grasp my sash of crimson.
Allow me to wash you innocent
in the Blood of my Lamb.
When you are washed in the Blood of my Lamb,
you have eyes to see me
in
the winds of change that embrace my earth.

Come to me now, little ones.
Come to the Lamb.
He gives you eyes that see Truth,
and
ears that hear the Voice of God once again.

I am your Lady of the Earth.
I am your Queen of Angels, dear angels
of my heart.
I am your Mother Most Pure.
Dwell in my heart, little children.
Dwell in my heart where Jesus lives.
In Jesus and through Jesus and with Jesus,
we are one, little children.

In Jesus, Heaven and earth meet.
In Jesus, all is made new.
Jesus is the New Heaven.
I am the New Earth.
Dwell in us, my little children of the earth.

Grasp my sash of crimson that you may
wear His Innocence in Purity,
my little children of the earth.
Wear the white of Innocence,
little ones, as you grasp my sash of crimson.

Arise, little ones.
Awaken from your slumber.
Sing to the Lamb.
Praise the Lamb.
Be like the Lamb.
Wash your hearts in the Blood of the Lamb.
Sing and dance and play in the New Earth,*
for
the old has passed away in the blink of an eye.
There, you experience the New Heaven.
There, you find Jesus forever.

Dear children of my heart,
the winds of change breathe lightly now.

---

*The means for this to happen is to "dwell" in the Immaculate Heart
by an Act of Consecration to the Immaculate Heart of Mary.

Soon gale forces shall drive from the earth
all that is not of my Son, for my Son, in my Son.
Thank you for your sacrifice to honor me.
Your life will bear sweet fruit for
my Son's Kingdom on earth.
God is reclaiming His earth.
Only those who are faithful shall live on.
There will be no others.

See the glories of God that lie hidden in each of
my precious children.

Cherish God's Faith in each of you.
Cherish God's Hope that each of you
will remain disciples
whom Jesus has loved into being.
Stand firm with me here on the earth
where my Son's Church has hung on the cross
for centuries.
Live in my Immaculate Heart, dear little children
of the Covenant,
for the winds of change are upon us.

My Son is a Faithful Son.
He rewards His Mother's children generously.
Know your prayers are answered,
but in ways that shall surprise you greatly.

You shall soon realize
that

the spiritual dark ages are ending
in
the shining Light of my Son Jesus' Presence
in the world.
Bless His Presence among you.

Awaken, little flock.
His glories are everywhere.
Awaken and drink of His Splendors.
Awaken and drink the Living Water.

"My soul proclaims the greatness of the
Lord; my spirit rejoices in God my savior,
For He has looked upon his servant's lowliness;
behold,
from now on will all ages call me blessed.
The Mighty One has done great things for
me, and holy is His name.
His mercy is from age to age to those who fear
him
according to His promise to our fathers,
to Abraham and to his descendants forever."

1) How I feel today:
Lord, thank You for another day on Your earth. I sensed Your nearness to me all day long and this has made me very happy. I feel filled with peace. Thank You, Lord.

2) Why I feel that way:
Dear Lord, whenever You are present in my conscious awareness, the warmth of Your love makes everything beautiful and filled with joy. Thank You for allowing me to be aware of Your presence in all that lives. Never allow me to lose that awareness.

3) Who and what I have encountered during the day and their effects on me:
Lord, thank You for the cold this morning. Though it was difficult to get out of bed, I offered my discomfort to You with hopes that it would be a small sign of my love for You. We haven't much money these days so I was happy to pass breakfast. The other members of the family need the food more than I do, and I felt happy to offer You another sign of my love for You. Lord, I do trust You to remedy our lack of money. You are the God of Providence and You do know what we need. Please open my eyes to every opportunity that passes my way this day to improve my family's well-being.

Lord, the traffic was snarled as I entered the freeway. I turned off the radio and tried to focus on Your presence throughout creation. Thank You, Lord, for that time to think of You. I know You think of me always. Help me to be more faithful to Your presence in me, around me, and with me. Help me to accept all the gifts You desire to give me.

4) An honest evaluation of how, where, and why God does or does not fit into my day and experiences.
Lord, people at work today were harassed and the mood was contagious. I quickly entered into the hassle, the frantic pace, and lost my peace. Did I create some of the confusion? Was I grumpy because I had not eaten? Perhaps I should have been kinder to my body and had at least some breakfast. Perhaps I am fooling myself that my "sacrifice" of food is pleasing to You. There is enough to eat in my home. I will not bypass breakfast again. Instead, I will abstain from sugar in my coffee as a small sacrifice. I will care for my body as Your temple. And I will try harder tomorrow to be "living peace" at work. I will no longer focus on my financial worries, Lord, but I will continue to work diligently and trust You to give me and my family all we need, and even more, for You are The Generous Heart.

5) A small personal prayer for Light.
Lord, You are the Light of the world and my personal Light. Thank You for Your patience with me. Grant me more faith and the patience to accept each moment as Your gift to me to grow in love, holiness, and abundance. Amen.

1) How I feel today:

Lord, You had to be consciously with me all day because I had a great day! Not a single thing went wrong! Thank you, Lord. I pray every day can be so great!

2) Why I feel that way:

I slept late because it is Saturday. Then I made breakfast for my family. It was wonderful to be together. We laughed and shared our week and made plans for next week. Every one is doing well. Thank you, Lord. Then I cleaned the garage. It was great fun, Lord. I am grateful to have a garage. I found lots of things I didn't know I had. Next weekend, we are going to have a real garage sale— the proceeds are for the party room for the disabled that we are building in our neighborhood. Thank you, Lord, for our disabled. They contribute in ways we cannot. I played golf this afternoon. What a great game I had! When I played to win instead of to enjoy Your presence in nature, I found golf stressful. Now, playing golf is an opportunity to walk eighteen holes and smile at Your interest in my recreation. My foursome can't believe how excellent my game is lately. You must be assigning your most athletic angels to my team. Thank you, Lord! I grilled outside for the family this evening. It was beautiful to be under your stars! Heaven seemed to be all around me. It has been a terrific day. I am grateful.

3) Who and what I have encountered during the day and their effects on me:
My spouse, children, and pets were all at home today. They washed the car while I cleaned the garage. Thank you for the car. My children are wonderful workers. It is great to work as a family. We laughed a lot. My spouse has a super sense of humor. My golf partners are faithful friends. I love their discipline. It helps me stay focused on what is important. The market was crowded when I did the shopping tonight. It is a blessing to be able to choose from such an array of foods from every area of the world. How blessed we are, Lord. Thank you! I'm hoping that it won't be long before all your people have the blessings I have. Please let me know what I can do to help. I'm going to read the Bible for a little while now, Lord. Please reveal Yourself to me in Your Word.

4) An honest evaluation of how, where, and why God does or does not fit into my day and my experiences.
I spent the entire day deeply connected to Your kindness, dear God. The wonderful people You have surrounded me with make my life interesting and challenging. The marvelous conveniences I have make my life quite pleasant. Thank You,

Lord. My concern is that I might forget the Source
of all this goodness around me. Please, Lord, never
let me take Your graciousness for granted.

A small personal prayer for Light.
Lord, please let me love, honor, and serve You always. Amen.

Selected Bibliography

Alocoque, Margaret Mary, Saint. *The Autobiography of Saint Margaret Mary.* Trans. V. Kerns. Westminster, MD: Newman Press, 1961.

Aquinas, Thomas. *The Catechetical Instructions.* Manila: Sinag-Talal Publishers, Inc., 1939.

———. *Summa Theologica.* 5 vols. Westminster, MD: Christian Classics, 1981.

———. *Summa Theologiae: A Concise Translation.* Westminster, MD: Christian Classics, 1989.

Aradi, Zsolt. *Shrines to Our Lady Around the World.* New York: Farrar, Straus and Young, 1954.

Auclair, Raoul. *The Lady of All People.* Trans. Earl Massecai. LacEtchmin, Quebec: L'Armée de Marie, 1978.

Augustine, Saint. *The Confessions.* Garden City, New York: Doubleday Image Books, 1960.

Barbaric, Slavko, O.F.M. *Fasting.* Steubenville, OH: Franciscan University Press, 1988.

———. *Pray with the Heart.* Steubenville, OH: Franciscan University Press, 1988.

Bateson, Mary Catherine. *Peripheral Vision.* New York: HarperCollins Publications, 1994.

Benkovic, Johnnette S. *Full of Grace.* Ann Arbor, MI: Servant Publications, 1998.

Bennett, William J. *The Book of Virtues.* New York: Simon and Schuster, 1993.

————. *The Death of Outrage.* New York: The Free Press, 1998.

Benson, Robert. *Living Prayer.* New York: Jeremy P. Tarcher/Putnam, 1998.

Bettwy, Sr. Isabel. *I Am the Guardian of the Faith.* Steubenville, OH: Franciscan University Press, 1991.

Bird, John. *Queen of the Ukraine.* Asbury, NJ. 101 Foundation, 1992.

Blackbourn, David. *Marpigen: Apparitions of the Virgin Mary in Nineteenth-century Germany.* New York: Alfred A. Knopf, 1994.

Bojorge, Horatio. *The Image of Mary According to the Evangelists.* New York: Alba House, 1978.

Boylan, M. Eugene. *This Tremendous Lover.* Allen, TX: Christian Classics, Inc., 1987.

Brigid, Saint. *The Magnificent Prayers of Saint Brigid of Sweden.* Rockford, IL: Tan Books, 1983.

Brigitta of Sweden, Saint. *Brigitta: Life and Selected Revelations.* New York: Paulist Press, 1990.

Brown, Michael H. *The Bridge to Heaven.* Lima, PA: Marian Communications, Ltd., 1993.

Bryant, Christopher. *The Heart in Pilgrimage.* New York: The Seabury Press, 1980.

Buono, Anthony. *Favorite Prayers to Our Lady.* New York: Catholic Book Publishing, 1991.

Burghardt, Walter, S.J. *Sir, We Would Like to See Jesus.* Ramsey, NJ: Paulist Press, 1982.

Burrows, Ruth. *Fire Upon the Earth*. Denville, NJ: Dimension Books, 1981.

Cahill, Thomas. *The Gift of the Jews*. New York: Doubleday, 1998.

Carter, Edward, S.J. *The Spiritually of Fatima and Medjugorje*. Milford, OH: Faith Publishing Co., 1994.

Cataneo, Pascal. *Padre Pio Gleanings*. Sherbrooke, QC: Editions Paulines, 1991.

Catherine of Geona, Saint. *Purgation and Purgatory: The Spiritual Dialogue*. New York: Paulist Press, 1979.

Catherine of Siena, Saint. *The Dialogue*. Ramsey, NJ: Paulist Press, 1980.

Caussade, Jean-Pierre de. *The Joy of Full Surrender*. Orleans, MA: Paraclete Press, 1986.

Ciszek, Walter, S.J. *With God in Russia*. Garden City, NY: Doubleday Image Books, 1966.

———. *He Leadeth Me*. San Francisco: Ignatius Press, 1997.

Connell, Janice T. *Queen of the Cosoms*. Introduction by Robert Faricy. Orleans, MA: Paraclete Press, 1990.

———. *The Visions of the Children*. Introduction by Robert Faricy. New York: St. Martin's Press, 1992.

———. *The Triumph of The Immaculate Heart*. Introduction by René Laurentin. Santa Barbara, CA: Queenship Publishing, 1993.

———. *Angel Power*. Introduction by Robert Faricy. New York: Ballantine Books, 1995.

———. *Meetings With Mary*. New York: Ballantine Books, 1995.

————. *Praying With Mary*. San Francisco: HarperSan-Francisco, 1997.

————. *The Visions of the Children*. Revised edition. Introduction by Robert Faricy. New York: St. Martin's Press, 1997.

————. *Prayer Power*. San Francisco: HarperSanFrancisco, 1998.

Danielou, Jean, S.J. *The Angels and Their Mission According to The Fathers of the Church*. Westminster, MD: Christian Classics, 1988.

Delaney, John J. *A Woman Clothed With the Sun*. New York: Doubleday Image Books, 1961.

De Waal, Esther. *Seeking God: The Way of St. Benedict*. London: HarperCollins Publishers, 1996.

Dossey, Larry, M.D. *Healing Words*. San Francisco: Harper, 1993.

Dubay, Thomas, S.M. *Fire Within*. San Francisco: Ignatius Press, 1989.

Dupre, Louis, and James A. Wiseman, editors. *Light From Light: An Anthology of Christian Mysticism*. New York: Paulist Press, 1988.

Duquesne, Jacques. *Jesus: An Unconventional Biography*. Liguori, MO: Triumph Books, 1997.

Eadie, Betty J. *Embraced By the Light*. Foreword by Melvin Morse, M.D. Placerville, CA: Gold Leaf Press, 1992.

Emmerich, Anne Catherine. *The Life of the Blessed Virgin Mary*. Rockford, IL: Tan Books, 1954.

Escriva, Blessed Josemaria. *The Way*. Manila: Sinag-Tala Publishers, Inc., 1982.

Estrade, J. B. *My Witness, Bernadette*. Springfield, IL: Templegate, 1946.

Faricy, Robert, S.J. *Praying For Inner Healing.* New York: Paulist Press, 1979.

———. *The Lord's Dealing: The Primacy of The Feminine in Christian Spiritually.* New York: Paulist Press, 1988.

Faricy, Robert, S.J., and Lucy Rooney, S.D.N. *The Contemplative Way of Prayer.* Ann Arbor, MI: Servant Books, 1986.

———. *Return to God: The Scottsdale Message.* Santa Barbara, CA: Queenship Publishing, 1993.

Fernandez-Carvajal, Francis, and Peter Beteta. *Children of God.* Princeton, NJ: Scepter Publishing, 1997.

Flynn, Ted and Maureen. *The Thunder of Justice.* Sterling, VA: MaxKol Communications, Inc., 1993.

Fowler, Nancy. *To Bear Witness That I Am the Living Son of God.* Newington, VA: Our Loving Mother's Children, 1992.

Francis of Assisi, Saint. *The Best From All His Works: Christian Classics Collection.* Nashville, TN: Thomas Nelson Publisher, 1989.

Francis and Clare. *Francis and Clare, The Complete Works.* Trans. R. J. Armstrong and I.C. Brady. New York: Paulist Press, 1982.

François, Robert. *O Children, Listen to Me.* Lindenhurst, NY: The Workers of Our Lady of Mount Carmel, 1980.

Fukushima, Mutano (Francis). *Akita: Spiritual Oasis of Japan.* Santa Barbara, CA: Queenship Publishing, 1994.

Gambero, Luigi. *Mary and the Fathers of the Church.* San Francisco: Ignatius Press, 1999.

Gertrude of Helfta. *The Herald of Divine Love*. New York: Paulist Press, 1993.

Gillett, H. M. *Shrines of Our Lady in England and Wales*. London: Samuel Walker, LTD, 1957.

Glenn, Msgr. Paul J. *A Tour of the Summa*. Rockford, IL: Tan Books, 1978.

Gobbi, Don Stefano. *To the Priests, Our Lady's Beloved Sons*. (11th ed.). Toronto, Ontario: Marian Movement of Priests, 1990.

Griffiths, Bede. *The Cosmic Revelation: The Hindu Way to God*. Springfield, IL: Templegate Publishers, 1983.

————. *Sacred Wisdom of the World*. London: Harper-Collins, 1994.

Groeschel, Benedict, C.F.R. *A Still Small Voice*. San Francisco: Ignatius Press, 1992.

Heine, Max. *Equipping Men for Spiritual Battle*. Ann Arbor, MI: Servant Books, 1993.

Hempsche, John. *Preparation for the End Times*. Chicago, IL: Claretian Missionaries Publications, 1992.

Hickey, James Cardinal. *Mary at the Foot of the Cross*. San Francisco: Ignatius Press, 1988.

Hinn, Benny. *Good Morning, Holy Spirit*. Nashville: Thomas Nelson Publishers, 1990.

Huber, George. *My Angel Will Go Before You*. Introduction by Cardinal Charles Journet. Westminster, MD: Christian Classics, 1988.

Ignatius of Loyola, Saint. *The Spiritual Exercises*. Trans. Anthony Mohola. New York: Doubleday Image Books, 1989.

————. *A Pilgrim's Journey: The Autobiography of Ignatius of Loyola*. Collegeville, MN: The Liturgical Press, 1991.

Jelly, Frederick M. *Madonna: Mary in the Catholic Tradition*. New Huntington, IN: Our Sunday Visitor Publishing Division, 1986.

John of the Cross, Saint. *Selected Writings*. Trans. Kieran Kavanaugh, O.C.D. New York: Paulist Press, 1987.

John Paul II, Pope. *Mary: God's Yes to Man*. Encyclical Letter *Mother of the Redeemer*. Introduction by Joseph Cardinal Ratzinger. San Francisco: Ignatius Press, 1988.

————. Encyclical Letter *The Splendor of Truth*. Boston: Saint Paul Books and Media, 1993.

————. *Crossing the Threshold of Hope*. New York: Alfred A. Knopf, 1994.

————. Apostolic Letter *Dies Domini*. Boston: Daughters of St. Paul, 1998.

————. Encyclical Letter *Fides et Ratio*. Boston: Daughters of St. Paul, 1998.

Johnson, Francis. *Fatima, The Great Sign*. Rockford, IL: Tan Books, 1980.

Johnson, William, ed. *The Cloud of Unknowing*. New York: Doubleday Image Books, 1973.

Julian of Norwich. *Showings*. Introduction by Edmund Cooledge, O.S.A., and James Walsh, S.J. New York: Paulist Press, 1978.

Keithley, June. *Lipa*. Manila: Anvil Publishing, 1992.

Kempis, Thomas a. *The Imitation of Christ in Four Books*. New York: Catholic Book Publishing Co., 1977.

Kondor, L., ed. *Fatima in Lucia's Own Words*. Trans. Dominican Nuns of the Perpetual Rosary. Fatima, Portugal: Postulation Centre, 1976.

Kowalska, Blessed M. Faustina. *Divine Mercy in My Soul: The Diary*. Stockbridge, MA: Marian Press, 1987.

Kunzli, Josef. *The Messages of Our Lady of All Nations.* Holland: Secretariat, 1987.

Langsam, Jude, managing ed. *Welcome to Carmel.* Washington, DC: Teresian Charism Press, 1982.

Laurentin, René. *Bernadette at Lourdes.* Minneapolis, MN: Winston Press, 1979.

———. *The Apparitions at Medjugorje Prolonged.* Trans. J. Lohre Stiens. Milford, OH: The Riehle Foundation, 1987.

———. *A Year of Grace with Mary.* Dublin, Ireland: Veritas Publications, 1987.

———. *The Church and Apparitions—Their Status and Function; Criteria and Reception.* Milford, OH: The Riehle Foundation, 1989.

———. *An Appeal From Mary in Argentina.* Milford, OH: The Riehle Foundation, 1990.

———. *The Apparitions of the Blessed Virgin Mary Today.* Dublin, Ireland: Veritas Publications, 1990.

———. *Our Lord and Our Lady in Scottsdale.* Milford, OH: Faith Publishing Co., 1992.

Laurentin, René, and H. Joyeux. *Scientific and Medical Studies on the Apparitions at Medjugorje.* Trans. L. Griffin. Dublin: Veritas, 1987.

Laurentin, René, and Lejeune. *Messages and Teachings of Mary at Medjugorje.* Milford, OH: The Riehle Foundation, 1988.

Lewis, C. S. *The Screwtape Letters.* New York: The Macmillan Company, 1943.

Liguori, Alphonsus de, Saint. *The Glories of Mary.* Rockford, IL: Tan Books, 1977.

Lucia, Visionary of Fatima. *Fatima in Lucia's Own Words.* Fatima, Portugal: Postulation Centre, 1976.

Lymann, Sanford M. *The Seven Deadly Sins: Society and Evil*. New York: St. Martin's Press, 1978.

MacDonald, Hope. *Traditional Values for Today's New Woman*. Grand Rapids, MI: Zondervan Publishing House, 1990.

Maloney, George A., S.J. *Called to Intimacy: Living in the Indwelling Presence*. New York: Alba House, 1983.

Margaret Mary, Saint. *The Autobiography*. Rockford, IL: Tan Publishers, 1952.

Mary of Agreda, The Venerable. *Mystical City of God*. 4 vols. Washington, NJ: Ave Maria Institute, 1971.

Mayer, Michael. *A Private Letter From Zuzuland*. Sacred Heart Parish: Inkamana Abbey; P/Bag x 9333; Vryheid.

McKenzie, John L., S.J. *Dictionary of the Bible*. Milwaukee: The Bruce Publishing Company, 1965.

McSorley, Richard, S.J. *New Testament Basis for Peace Making*. Scottsdale, PA: Herald Press, 1985.

Michel, Frère de la Sainte Trinité. *The Whole Truth About Fatima*. Buffalo, NY: Immaculate Heart Publications, 1989.

Miravalle, Mark I., S.T.D., ed. *The Apostolate of Holy Motherhood*. Milford, OH: The Riehle Foundation, 1991.

———. *The Message of Medjugorje*. Lanham, MD: University Press of America, 1986.

———. *Introduction to Mary*. Santa Barbara, CA: Queenship Publishing, 1993.

———. *Mary: Coredemptrix, Mediatrix, Advocate*. Santa Barbara, CA: Queenship Publishing, 1993.

Mohr, Sister Marie Helene, S.C. *Saint Philomina, Powerful with God*. Rockford, IL: Tan Books, 1988.

Montfort, Louis Grignon de, Saint. *True Devotion to Mary,* ed. *The Fathers of the Company of Mary.* Trans. F. W. Faber. Rockford, IL: Tan Books, 1941.

———. *The Secret of the Rosary.* Washington, NJ: The Blue Army, 1951.

———. *God Alone: The Collected Writings of St. Louis de Montfort.* Washington, NJ: The Blue Army, 1989.

———. *The Secrets of Mary.* Rockford, IL: Tan Books, 1998.

Moore, Thomas. *Care of the Soul.* New York: Harper Collins, 1992.

Morse, Melvin, M.D. *Transformed by the Light.* New York: Ivy Books, 1992.

Most, William G. *Our Father's Plan.* Manassas, VA: Trinity Communications, 1988.

Mowatt, Archpriest John J. *The Holy and Miraculous Icon of Our Lady of Kazan.* Fatima, Portugal: Domus Pacis, 1974.

Mullins, Peter. *Shrines of Our Lady.* Foreword by Janice T. Connell. New York: St. Martin's Press, 1998.

Muto, Susan A. *Pathways of Spiritual Living.* Garden City, NY: Doubleday Image Books, 1984.

National Conference of Catholic Bishops. *Behold Your Mother: A Pastoral Letter on the Blessed Virgin Mary.* Washington, DC: United States Catholic Conference, Nov. 21, 1973.

Neumann, Erich. *The Great Mother.* Trans. Ralph Mannheim. Princeton, NJ: Princeton University Press, 1955.

Newman, John Henry. *Mary the Second Eve.* Rockford, IL: Tan Books, 1982.

Nikodimos, Saint, and Saint Makarios of Corinth. *The Philokalia.* 4 vols. London: Faber and Faber, 1984.

Northcote, J. *Celebrated Sanctuaries of the Madonna.* London: Longmans Green, 1968.

O'Carroll, Michael, C.C.Sp. *Theotokos: A Theological Encyclopedia of the Blessed Virgin Mary.* Wilmington, DE: Michael Glazier, 1982.

————. *Medjugorje Facts, Documents, Theology.* Dublin: Veritas, 1986.

O'Connor, Edward D., C.S.C. *The Catholic Vision.* Huntington, IN: Our Sunday Visitor Publishing Division, 1992.

Odell, Catherine M. *Those Who Saw Her: The Apparitions of Mary.* Huntington, IN: Our Sunday Visitor Press, 1986.

Opus Sanctorum Angelorum. *Newsletter.* Casa Regina Pacis / Rua do Anjo, 5. 2495 Fatima, Portugal. Tel.: (049) 532280. Fax.: (049) 531172.

Origen. *An Exhortation to Martyrdom, Prayer, First Principles: Book IV.* New York: Paulist Press, 1979.

Pelletier, Joseph. *The Sun Danced at Fatima.* Garden City, NY: Image Books, 1951.

————. "The Fatima Secret in 1960?" *The Messenger of the Sacred Heart* 95 (January 1960): 18–22.

————. *Our Lady Comes to Garabandal, Including Concita's Diary.* Worcester, MA: Assumption Publications, 1971.

————. *The Queen of Peace Visits Medjugorje.* Worcester, MA: Assumption Publications, 1985.

Petrisko, Thomas W. *Calls of the Ages.* Santa Barbara, CA: Queenship Publishing, 1995.

Pius XI, Pope. *Ineffabilis Deus.* December 8, 1854.

Pius XII, Pope. *Signa Magna*. Encyclical Letter, 1948.

———. *Munificentissimus Deus*. 1950.

Prince, Derek. *Blessing or Curse: You Can Choose*. Tarrytown, NY: Chosen Books, 1990.

Publican, The. *The Miracle of Damascus*. Glendale, CA: The Messengers of Unity, 1989.

Reck, William A. *Thoughts on Apparitions*. Milford, OH: The Riehle Foundation, 1993.

Rengers, Christopher. *The Youngest Prophet*. New York: Alba House, 1986.

Roberts, Cokie. *We Are Our Mothers' Daughters*. New York: William Morrow and Company, 1998.

Rouvelle, Alexander de. *Imitation of Mary in Four Books*. New York: Catholic Book Publishing, 1985.

Sales, Francis de, Saint. *The Sermons of Saint Francis De Sales on Our Lady*, ed. Lewis S. Fiorelli. Rockford, IL: Tan Books, 1985.

Sanford, Agnes. *The Healing Gifts of the Spirit*. Philadelphia: Harper and Row, 1966.

Sanford, John A. *The Kingdom Within*. San Francisco: Harper and Row, 1987.

Scanlan, Michael, T.O.R. *Appointment With God*. Steubenville, OH: Franciscan University Press, 1987.

Scanlan, Michael, and Randall J. Cirner. *Deliverance From Evil Spirits*. Ann Arbor, MI: Servant Books, 1980.

Schlessinger, Laura, and Rabbi Stewart Vogel. *The Ten Commandments*. New York: Cliff Street Books, 1998.

Schouppe, F. X., S.J. *The Dogma of Hell*. Rockford, IL: Tan Books and Publishers, 1989.

Scupoli, Dom Lorenzo. *The Spiritual Combat and a Treatise on Peace of Soul.* Rockford, IL: Tan Books and Publishers, 1990.

Shamon, Albert. *The Power of the Rosary.* Milford, OH: The Riehle Foundation, 1989.

Sheen, Fulton J. *Three to Get Married.* Princeton, NJ: Scepter Publishing, 1951.

Silvestrini, Achille. *The Life of the Madonna in Art.* Boston, MA: Daughters of Saint Paul, 1985.

Sims, Sister Margaret Catherine. *Apparitions in Betania, Venezuela.* Framingham, MA: Medjugorje Messengers, 1992.

Singer, Jim Z. *Use My Gifts: The Messages of Our Lord.* Toronto, Canada: Ave Maria Center of Peace, 1993.

Sreavinskas, Oeter M.J., ed. *Catholic Encyclopedia.* Huntington, IN: Our Sunday Visitor, 1991.

Sullivan, Gianna Talone. *I AM Your Jesus of Mercy.* 3 vols. Milford, OH: The Riehle Foundation, 1989.

————. *I AM Your Jesus of Mercy.* Vol. 4. Santa Barbara, CA: Queenship Publishing, 1993.

Supple, David, O. S. B., ed. *Virgin Wholly Marvelous.* Cambridge: The Ravengate Press, 1981.

Terelya, Josyp, with Michael Brown. *Josyp Terelya Witness.* Milford, OH: Faith Publishing Company, 1991.

Theresa of Avila, St. *The Way of Perfection.* Trans. and ed. Allison Peers. New York: Doubleday Image Books, 1964.

————. *The Interior Castle.* Trans. K. Kavanaugh. New York: Paulist Press, 1979.

————. *Collected Works.* 3 vols. Trans. K. Kavanaugh and O. Rodriguez. Washington, DC: ICS Publications, 1985.

Therese, Saint of Lisieux. *The Autobiography: The Story of a Soul.* New York: Doubleday, 1957.

Tissot, Jospeh. *How to Profit from One's Faults.* London: Scepter, 1996.

Two Friends of Medjugorje. *Words From Heaven.* Birmingham, AL: St. James Publishing, 1990.

Van Kaam, Adrian, C.S.Sp. *The Mystery of Transforming Love.* Denville, NJ: Dimension Books, Inc., 1981.

————. *The Roots of Christian Joy.* Denville, NJ: Dimension Books, Inc., 1985.

Vincent, R. *Please Come Back to Me and My Son.* Lynn Industrial Estate, Mullingar, Co. Westmeath: Ireland's Eye Publications, 1992.

Wagner, E. Glenn. *The Awesome Power of Shared Beliefs.* Dallas, TX: Word Publishing, 1995.

Walsh, Michael, ed. *Butler's Lives of the Saints.* Foreword by Cardinal Basil Hume. San Francisco: Harper and Row, 1984.

Walsh, William J., ed. *The Apparitions and Shrines of Heaven's Bright Queen.* 4 vols. New York: T. J. Carey, 1904.

Weible, Wayne. *Medjugorje: The Message.* Orleans, MA: Paraclete Press, 1989.

Weil, Simone. *Waiting for God.* New York: Harper and Row, 1951.

Werfel, Franz. *The Song of Bernadette.* Trans. Ludwig Lewisohn. New York: Saint Martin's Press, 1970.

Wright, Cardinal John. *Mary Our Hope.* San Francisco: Ignatius Press, 1988.

Wyszynski, Cardinal Stefan. *Working Your Way into Heaven*. Manchester, NH: Sophia Institute Press, 1995.

Yasuda, Teiji. *Akita: The Tears and Message of Mary*. English version by John Haffert. Asbury, NJ: 101 Foundation, 1989.

Zimdals-Swartz, Sandra L. *Encountering Mary from LaSalette to Medjugorje*. Princeton, NJ: Princeton University Press, 1991.

Zovko, Jozo, O.F.M. *A Man Named Father Jozo*. Milford, OH: The Riehle Foundation, 1989.

Afterword

Mary, greeting her pregnant cousin Elizabeth, and carrying Jesus in her womb, says,
"My soul magnifies the Lord,
My spirit is glad in God my savior;
Because He has looked with favor
On the lowliness of His servant."

Mary magnifies God. She glorifies Him, praises Him, gives Him glory. Mary acts as a focus for the Lord, in analogy with a magnifying glass that focuses the sun's rays. Praise results, praise that glorifies, magnifies God. Why? Because she is humble before the Lord. Considering herself a servant, a handmaid, Mary lowers herself, humbles herself. She stands humble before the Lord in the truth of her own existence: that she depends entirely on God and on His merciful love for her. She depends on the Lord for her very existence, for her role as the Mother of Jesus, for everything. The recognition in Mary's heart of this reality, of this factual state of affairs, is her humility, her lowliness.

Clear from the Gospels, and manifest in the entire Christian tradition of writing and painting, is this: Mary's outstanding quality, her great virtue, is her humility before God, her openness, her transparency before the Lord. The highest of human beings, because she is the Mother of God, comes to Elizabeth and to everyone, including God, as the lowest, the most humble. The first becomes the lowest, the last. And that is why she is the first, why she finds favor with God. The Lord looks on Mary with favor because she is lowly.

Mary's humility before God comes from her knowledge of her creatureliness. Even though sinless from her conception, even though the Mother of God, Mary remains completely a creature. Not divine in any way, not at all God, but the highest and holiest of creatures, higher and holier than even the angels.

Mary is Queen of Angels, over the angels, and even closer to God than the angels. And, at the same time, she is our Mother. Not just the Mother of us all. That too. But, in particular, the Mother of each one of us.

Mary is the Mother of Jesus. That is to say, God came to us as a human, as Jesus, first through Mary, conceived in her womb. Mary is the Mother of Jesus. And the relationship of motherhood is permanent. Your mother is always your mother, even after you have been born, brought up, and perhaps left home. Even after death. Mary is still Jesus' Mother.

And because Mary is still Jesus' Mother, because the relationship is permanent, He still comes to us through her. And so the life of the Spirit, the life of grace, the life that Jesus pours into our hearts, always comes to us through Mary. That makes Mary the Mother of each one of us in the spiritual order, the Spiritual Mother of each one of us, my Mother and your Mother.

Does that mean I have to go to Jesus through Mary? No. It means that I can. I can go to Mary, because she is my Mother, personally, calling me by name, giving me her full attention and her love.

When Jesus began his public ministry, at the wedding reception in the town of Cana of Galilee, He said he was not ready to begin. He had not yet called all the apostles, He was not ready to begin his ministry of preaching, of healing, and of helping people by working miracles. John's Gospel tells us what happened:

There was a wedding in the town of Cana, in Galilee. Jesus' mother was present, and Jesus and His followers were there, too. They ran out of wine, and the Mother of Jesus said to Him, "They have no more wine." He answered her, "What is that to us? My time has not yet come." Jesus' Mother said to the servants, "Do whatever he tells you." Standing near were six stone jars, the kind used for Jewish rituals of purification. Each jar could hold twenty or thirty gallons of water. Jesus told the servants, "Fill the jars with water." They filled up the jars. "Now pour some out," Jesus said, "and take it to the master of ceremonies." They did this. The master of ceremonies tasted the water, now turned into wine; he did not know where the wine came from, but the servants knew. The master of ceremonies called the bridegroom, and said to him, "People serve the best wine first, and the less good wine later, when people have had more to drink; but you have kept the best wine until the last!" Jesus did this first one of His signs in Cana, in Galilee, and so He revealed His glory, and His followers believed in Him.

What can we learn from this? Mary, with complete trust in Jesus, asked Him to solve the problem. Jesus did what Mary asked, even though He said it was not yet His time for performing a miracle as a sign. Jesus acted not only because His Mother asked Him but also out of compassion for the bride and groom and their parents, helping them so that they would not be embarrassed at not having enough wine for the wedding feast.

What happened at the wedding at Cana serves as a model, a paradigm, for us. Mary wants to help us, intercede for us, get Jesus to help us, mother us, look after us. We can turn to her.

She is with God, totally. After her death, Mary, the Mother of Jesus, was taken up to heaven, to be there with Jesus and to be there for

us. For me and for you. To be the Spiritual Mother of each one of us.

Jan Connell, the author of this book, knows the Mother of Jesus. This book will help a lot of people throughout the world of every culture, faith, and nation.

—*Robert Faricy, S.J.*
Professor of Mystical Theology
Gregorian University, Rome